THE WAR ON
SUCCESS

THE WAR ON
SUCCESS

HOW THE OBAMA AGENDA IS
SHATTERING THE AMERICAN DREAM

TOMMY NEWBERRY

Since 1947
REGNERY
PUBLISHING, INC.
An Eagle Publishing Company • Washington, DC

Cataloging-in-Publication data on file with the Library of Congress

ISBN 978-1-59698-118-8

Published in the United States by
Regnery Publishing, Inc.
One Massachusetts Avenue, NW
Washington, DC 20001
www.regnery.com

Manufactured in the United States of America

10 9 8 7 6 5 4 3 2 1

Books are available in quantity for promotional or premium use. Write to Director of Special Sales, Regnery Publishing, Inc., One Massachusetts Avenue NW, Washington, DC 20001, for information on discounts and terms or call (202) 216-0600.

Distributed to the trade by:
Perseus Distribution
387 Park Avenue South
New York, NY 10016

CONTENTS

This book is dedicated to the children of America,
who will inherit the nation we leave behind.

AN OPEN LETTER TO PRESIDENT OBAMA

Dear Mr. President,

I HAVE THE HIGH HONOR AND DISTINCT PRIVILEGE of writing to you on behalf of millions of leading entrepreneurs, small business owners, salespeople, and executives whose creativity, work ethic, and personal responsibility make up the backbone of the American economic engine and therefore keep the American Dream alive.

These individuals have become highly paid because they are highly productive. For some reason, however, you do not refer to these Americans as "working people"—you typically call them "the rich." But with all due respect Mr. President, they work indeed, often putting in sixty, seventy, and even eighty hour weeks in order to satisfy their customers and expand their businesses.

These are the most successful Americans who create vast numbers of jobs. And yet, contrary to your campaign promises of "hope" for all Americans, you have singled them out for condemnation and expropriation. You say we need to spread their wealth around in the interests of fairness. You vow to make them pay higher taxes, even though they already pay far more than anyone else. You bury their businesses in a morass of red-tape and useless regulation. You attempt to make the government—instead of their customers—the arbiter of their success.

Mr. President, I am writing to ask that you STOP THE WAR ON SUCCESS!

I have been working with entrepreneurs and small business owners and their families for nearly twenty years. The picture you paint of the free market, the business world, and successful business owners is totally foreign to me. You speak of successful Americans as if they're all corrupt corporate CEOs. Do you not understand that many of the very people you denounce are small businessmen and businesswomen who earned their own wealth?

You speak of a rich man as selfish, but do you see the jobs he has created? You speak of him as having more than he needs, but did you see how little he had when he accepted the risk of starting his own business? You speak of luck, but did you see the years of misfortune that preceded his success? You speak of him as "privileged," but have you heard that fewer than 20 percent of rich Americans inherited their wealth?

I have seen firsthand that these individuals have unbelievable work ethics and the highest integrity. Imaginative and innovative, they create jobs out of thin air. They treat their employees like family. They are compassionate and giving and donate a greater percentage of their income to churches and charities than public records reveal most of our elected officials do, including you and your vice president. Many have failed repeatedly, and yet they get back up and take another shot at excellence.

Mr. President, I do not know what it's like to be a community organizer. I have no firsthand experience so I will keep my mouth shut and my pen silent on such matters. It is impossible to expect you, as president, to remain equally quiet about business matters. But perhaps your utter lack of experience in this realm should be cause for some humility. You have not taken the risks of starting and growing your own business or participating in the free marketplace at all. You do not understand what business really is; it is certainly not what you present it to be.

One can fairly ask why your commitment to spreading the wealth around only applies to business—and not to politics. For example, shouldn't it apply to your position of President of the United States? By achieving this position, you have attained disproportionate status and power in your field. In politics, you are the "super-rich." So shouldn't you spread your political wealth around to those who have not been as fortunate as you? Doesn't your enthusiasm for "redistributive justice" mean some of your enormous power should be taken from you and given to others who have less power?

This, no doubt, will sound ludicrous to you, as you worked hard for many years to get where you are today. Why should you have to give away the fruits of your own success? In your mind, it is only the entrepreneur whose success should be expropriated and spread around. The politically powerful, like yourself, are mysteriously exempt from the demands of equality.

Finally Mr. President, consider the message you are sending to America's young people. I truly believe our greatest generations are still to come, but it will never happen if our children believe the messages transmitted by your rhetoric and policies: that no one can succeed on their own, that business is fundamentally dishonorable and dishonest, that only the government can save us from the depredations of businessmen and businesswomen, and that anyone who is financially successful is a societal parasite.

The entrepreneurial class you demonize is largely responsible for America's high standard of living and its unprecedented pace of technological innovation. Think about the consequences of your relentless attack on these people and everything they represent—success, prosperity, upward mobility, and self-sufficiency. Whether through your rhetoric of class warfare or through your policies of expropriation and redistribution, you are undermining this vital group of Americans. America may indeed become more equal without these entrepreneurs, but it will be the equality of poverty and mediocrity, of underachievement and apathy.

And now I ask you, Mr. President: where's the hope in that?

Sincerely,
Tommy Newberry

CHAPTER ONE

THREAT LEVEL RED

"Freedom is never more than one generation away from extinction. We didn't pass it to our children in the bloodstream. It must be fought for, protected, and handed on for them to do the same, or one day we will spend our sunset years telling our children and our children's children what it was once like in the United States where men were free."

—PRESIDENT RONALD REAGAN

AMERICA IS UNDER ATTACK.
Ambushed at the height of economic vulnerability, many Americans are still frozen with fear. Our own government has launched an undeclared war that aims to extinguish the American spirit and destroy the American Dream. Out of fear many have not even fought back.

This war, the War on Success, is not just an economic war on the so-called "rich"—Barack Obama's vow to "spread the wealth around" is just the tip of the iceberg. The War on Success is an invasive battle against ambition, personal responsibility, and individual achievement, for these virtues compete with the priorities of the current administration. It is an assault on traditional values and a cultural war against the things we hold dear. It is an aggressive affront on the productive, the traditional, and the principled. Ultimately, it is an attack on America's founding principles and on free enterprise. It is a war that threatens the very character of this nation.

The War on Success is being waged for the sake of seductive, vague, and emotion-provoking terms such as "fairness," "justice," and "compassion." But the real goal is to undermine the American spirit of independent entrepreneurship in order to expand the role of the government—in the economy overall, as well as in our everyday lives. A bigger, more coercive, more intrusive government is what our opponents seek. The free market is deemed too chaotic, too unpredictable, and too unfair. From big issues like healthcare to minute ones like what's on our dinner plates, government planners think they can do a better job of managing our choices for us—if we only surrender our independent initiative to them.

This war aims to abolish our nation's traditional model of success, grounded in Judeo-Christian virtues and the founding principles of our country. The Founders intended a nation where the citizens could both sow and reap free of unnatural interference from government. But the Obama administration envisions a nation where the government controls and manipulates the reaping.

This unnecessary conflict can be boiled down to two common words: *from* and *through*. President Obama believes in freedom *through* government. This is complex, messy, and unattainable in the long run. The government, at its discretion, reaches onto a person's land and takes the harvest he produced with his labor and transfers this "success" to a fellow citizen of its choosing. In other words, some individuals get what they want through the government's intervention. Freedom in this sense refers to entitlement. This concept was aptly described by the American philosopher Eric Hoffer: "To the frustrated, freedom from responsibility is more attractive than freedom from restraint. They are eager to barter their independence for relief from the burdens of willing, deciding, and being responsible for inevitable failure. They willingly abdicate the directing of their lives to those who want to plan, command, and shoulder all responsibility."[1]

In contrast, the formula of America's Founders is freedom *from* government. This is straightforward and achievable. This means an individual can pursue what he wants without government interference. We plant, we nurture, and we reap the harvest ourselves. Freedom in this sense refers to opportunity.

In the traditional American model, one earns his success on his own merit through personal initiative, resourcefulness, value creation, and persistence. But the War on Success seeks to abolish the concept of merit so that the government awards "success" to the people the state deems deserving of it. These elevated cliques of "more deserving" people become loyal constituent groups who get the things they want as a matter of public policy, independent of whether or not they earned them. The politicians who arrange these economic favors can then sit back and relax on election night—or more accurately, on re-election night.

The War on Success was not announced candidly to the American public, but it has been repeatedly and brazenly affirmed and documented in both speech and policy by the President of the United States and his top administration officials. This war attacks the following American virtues:

1. Limited government
2. Individualism
3. Free enterprise
4. Fiscal responsibility
5. Private ownership
6. The Constitution

In waging the War on Success, the Obama administration and its allies portray America as an inherently unfair, unjust country where only the corrupt and the connected succeed. Their rhetoric is suffused with themes of class warfare, condemning America's most successful, productive citizens as "selfish," "greedy," and "lucky." The "rich" are demonized and ostracized in order to pave the way for policies that expropriate and redistribute their wealth—and increasingly, to pave the way for the government to take over their entire companies. The "rich" are making too much money, we're told, as Congress debates one proposal after another to raise taxes on them and limit their salaries. Business itself is also roundly condemned; we are constantly told that America needs more and more regulation so the government can stop greedy companies from exploiting their customers.

What's underway in Washington is not a slight tinkering or a fine-tuning of our free market system. Rather, in his Inaugural Address, President Obama announced his intention to "remake America."[2] This was no offhand comment; a few months later, the president affirmed, "We have begun the work of remaking America."[3] These statements should disturb Americans of any party affiliation—America was made through Judeo-Christian values and free enterprise. Any fundamental "remaking" of the nation would require abandoning one or both of these traditions.

These declarations are a key weapon in the War on Success. Americans must be convinced through sheer rhetoric that contrary to this nation's entire history of bold, creative entrepreneurship, it is impossible for anyone to succeed by virtue of his own labor and ingenuity. Obama's campaign speeches may have revolved around "hope," but hope will only appear after he's done "remaking" America. In the current system, there is no hope—the "rich" and their evil businesses supposedly ensure that. The only way to succeed, we are led to believe, is for the government to provide success to us.

In reality, success is only meaningful because it is *not* guaranteed. Like the U.S. Marine motto, true success "is earned, never given"—no politician in either party can provide any of us with the life we really deserve.

We must not be deceived; we are at risk of losing that which is unique and distinctive about America. Our government is embarking on a radical project of social leveling in which the best and the brightest are deliberately cut down into the mediocre and the bland. We are on a path to join Europe in a steady, irreversible decline. Reduced to a state of perpetual irrelevancy, Europeans find no interest in either procreation or innovation. Can you name the last breakthrough originating in Europe that has improved the quality of your life? With no legacy to leave behind and little faith in the future, most Europeans are sheepishly content to have their behavior regulated and their quality of life guaranteed with cradle-to-grave welfare.

This future has now been chosen for us as well.

THE STATIST TEMPTATION

This war is being waged by people who place the interests of the government over individual liberties. Their philosophy has existed for many years, though it mutates over time and according to local conditions. It has taken the brutal forms of communism and fascism, as well as lighter incarnations like American "progressivism" and the "social democracy" that currently dominates western Europe. Regardless of their particular ideology, its adherents oppose America's traditions of capitalism, maximum political freedom, and rugged individualism.

These people are called statists.

Relying on emotional appeals rather than reason and logic, statists disdain fixed principles and deny the existence of absolute truths. They define morality in political terms—whatever advances their political agenda is deemed to be good. They don't have faith in individuals, in business, or in God. They have faith in one thing: government.

BE STREET-SMART:
MASTER THE STATIST VOCABULARY LIST

CAPITALISM: the deliberate exploitation of the poor and middle class by the wealthy

COMMON GOOD: the supremacy of the collective over the rights of the individual; "good" is determined and enforced by the state

ECONOMIC JUSTICE: the establishment of uniform economic outcomes

ENVY: the natural human response to social and economic injustice

EQUALITY: see "fairness," "social justice," "economic justice," "freedom," and "common good"

EQUAL RIGHTS: see "special rights"

FAIRNESS: equality; uniformity of result; see also "social justice" and "economic justice"

FREEDOM: deliverance by government from disagreeable conditions and most grievances and burdens

GREED: see "selfish," "profit," and "capitalism"

PROFIT: ill-gotten gains from the exploitation of the working class

REDISTRIBUTION: taking from the selfish and transferring to the exploited

SACRIFICE: when the responsible citizen pays for the mistakes of the irresponsible citizen

SELFISH: those who resist the transfer of their earnings to strangers

SOCIALIST: someone who has lots of ideas for using other people's money

SOCIAL JUSTICE: another name for the pursuit of equal results; see also "economic justice"

continued

---

continued

SPECIAL RIGHTS: additional rights and protections for specific demographic groups; usually called "equal rights"

STATIST: one who believes in the superiority of the government over individual citizens; believes the state acts in the best interest of the collective good

STIMULUS: massive expansion of government

WORN-OUT DOGMAS: the Constitution, limited government, liberty, individualism, and capitalism

---

America has been flirting with statism for decades, but this relationship has become uncomfortably intimate with the election of Barack Obama, a statist extraordinaire. Consider the current state of the Union. Right now, our government is running, controlling, or exerting its heavy hand on banks, mortgage lenders, car manufacturers, and insurance companies. It has ratcheted up government spending to unprecedented, unsustainable levels, saddling future generations with a crushing debt. This administration also plans to raise taxes for entrepreneurs and small business owners,[4] and raise billions more through disguised taxes on American consumers, such as the proposed cap-and-trade scheme. Oil, coal, and natural gas companies that provide the fuel of our economic engine are being subject to increasingly untenable levels of government regulation—with Obama vowing that cap-and-trade will "bankrupt" any power company that builds a new coal plant.

On a personal level, this administration aims to bring about a far more intrusive government. Through environmental regulation, it hungers to control the choice of car we drive and the amount of energy we use in our home. Through healthcare "reform," it is trying to establish a bigger government role in deciding which doctor we visit, what treatment we receive, and what goes in our medicine cabinet. Through attempts to resurrect the Fairness Doctrine, it wants to control what is said over the airwaves and who gets to say it.

And that's just the quick overview!

Make no mistake—more than anything else, the statist has an unquenchable lust for control, for dictating how we run our lives, how we raise our families, and how we operate our businesses. Whatever the problem or grievance, you can count on the statist to propose a "solution" with the liberal convenience of other people's money. However, giving the government more power is like handing over the car keys to a teenage boy along with a bottle of Jack Daniels. We won't like how the story ends. Why doesn't everyone see that the more our government has grown, the more our problems have grown?

The statist is like a neighborhood busybody, but with unrivaled coercive power. It's time we, loudly and clearly, tell government to MIND YOUR OWN BUSINESS!

Statism is aided and abetted by three powerful forces:

- Ignorance of the principles that make an individual and a country great
- Apathy—indifference born out of complacency
- Counterfeit compassion—excessive emotion-based decision making, corresponding with the suppression of reason and logic.

Working in tandem, these three forces are fracturing the nation's foundations, creating moral confusion, and allowing the statist philosophy to flood in and dilute the principles that matter most. According to Scottish historian Alexander Tytler,

> The average age of the world's greatest civilizations from the beginning of history, has been about 200 years. During those

200 years, these nations always progressed through the following sequence:

From bondage to spiritual faith;
From spiritual faith to great courage;
From courage to liberty;
From liberty to abundance;
From abundance to complacency;
From complacency to apathy;
From apathy to dependence;
From dependence back into bondage.[5]

This indeed appears to be our current trajectory. There is nothing
inevitable about our national decline, though: complacency, apathy, and dependence are not normal features of the American
character. Instead, these destructive traits are being deliberately
instilled in us by those who want to see a more powerful government preside over a less free American citizenry. This is the particular danger of American statists today: they don't resort to
force of arms or any other head-on attack. Instead, they insidi-
ously subvert America from within, undermining our national
self-confidence and our individual ambition through their gradual, invisible War on Success.

WHY I WROTE THIS BOOK

For two decades, I have devoted my life to figuring out what separates the successful from the unsuccessful, the winners from the
losers. After working with more than a thousand entrepreneurs
and their families in over thirty industries, I have come to understand how valuable these individuals are to this country. Naturally,
I became alarmed by then-candidate Barack Obama's divisive
rhetoric and his subsequent punitive policy proposals.

The story of President Obama is a true American success story, and one that is still in the making. He's passionate about his values and beliefs. He's ambitious, focused, and determined to achieve his objectives. In barely more than four years, Obama has gone from the Illinois state senate, to the United States Senate, to the American presidency. And with that last distinction, he's carved out another slot in the history books as America's first African-American president at the young age of forty-seven.

This is impressive indeed! Who would not admire someone who sets big goals and ends up reaching them? In fact, I have high regard for anyone who has the audacity to strive for an ambitious goal, even if he ultimately falls short of the mark. And in addition to reaching the highest political position in America, from all media accounts, Obama appears to be a friendly person, a fine husband, and a committed father to his two daughters.

Barack Obama has something I've found, in my research over the last twenty years, is common in the most successful people in all walks of life: he has what others label as "unrealistic goals." These are simply goals other people assumed could not be attained. But big thinkers launch out anyway, in spite of the long odds. America is filled with big thinkers and big doers like Obama, although most are not in the political arena and most are not household names.

In short, Obama shows many of the personal qualities that I admire most. That's why I was so taken aback by his anti-business outlook, his blind faith in government, and his intention to "remake" America. After succeeding on his own virtues, he declares that none of the rest of us can do it, and that the country must be fundamentally transformed to achieve "fairness."

I never aspired to write a political book. But the onset of the War on Success deeply affected me, since I have dedicated my life to the opposite idea: that *Success Is Not an Accident*, as I titled my first book. The War on Success struck me as a repudiation of the American Dream that countless Americans—including Obama himself—have actually achieved. As I talked over these ideas, numerous friends urged me to write a book defending free enterprise and the merit-based society. Others, however, warned me of the risks of alienating or offending people with my blunt observations and unambiguous convictions.

I decided to take the risk of writing this book after considering the sheer magnitude of the threat we face. The War on Success threatens to wash away our liberties, our way of life, and the limitless possibilities that have always characterized the American identity. It is especially important to draw attention to this threat when it's presented by an administration that has amassed unprecedented power and enacted sweeping changes in a breathtakingly short period of time. Dissent, as we repeatedly heard during the last administration, is the highest form of patriotism.

Here's what's driving me:

- Timeless principles are being ignored in favor of fashionable theories that have produced nothing but failure and mediocrity everywhere they have been implemented.

- There is an appalling lack of genuine debate about the root causes of our national problems and challenges. Instead, we focus on merely treating the symptoms, thereby postponing real solutions to a future generation.

- I believe this nation can reclaim its heritage if enough critically thinking citizens get fully engaged in standing up, speaking out, and warding off the stubborn strain of statist philosophy that has tainted so many in positions of authority today.

In this book, I aim to burst the bubble of complexity and reveal the simplicity and certainty of time-tested principles and how they relate to what is happening in America today. In doing this, I run the risk of criticism from the sophisticated intellectuals in politics, academia, and the media who reflexively scoff at such common-sense observations and solutions. The reader should note, however, that it's these "deep thinkers" who have led us into the economic and cultural muck through which we are now trudging. We, as a nation, have vested enormous power in an individual who has no track record in managing a business or creating jobs, and who has surrounded himself with many officials who would never have been hired if they were competing for their positions in the free marketplace instead of the political arena.

It is these people who are now attempting to "remake" our country.

TIME FOR ACTION

We are faced with a stark choice: to sit by passively and watch America decline, or to get off the sidelines, get in the game, and act now to preserve our way of life.

The time has come to aggressively defend free enterprise, individual success, and traditional American values. We have to stand up and fight for our children and grandchildren. This is a battle of ideas and principles, and we must approach it with a solemn sense of duty to future generations. We have been entrusted with the greatest country in the history of civilization, and we must now stand up and defend what is distinctive about her. Principles matter, and we must act fast to protect the principles that matter most. It is a responsibility we must accept and a calling we must answer. As Ralph Waldo Emerson wrote, "Nature has made up her mind that what cannot defend itself shall not be defended."[6]

My goal is to prepare you and other patriots to fight for your convictions and for this country's founding principles. We now have a higher calling, a mission to maneuver America back in the direction the Founders intended. We should take inspiration from Ronald Reagan's admonition: "You and I have a rendezvous with destiny. We will preserve for our children this, the last best hope of man on earth, or we will sentence them to take the first step into a thousand years of darkness. If we fail, at least let our children and our children's children say of us we justified our brief moment here. We did all that could be done."

Alternatively, we can let this nation continue to drift away from God, away from the Founders, away from principle, away from individual success, and toward a secular, ordinary, declining state, like a digital copy of our friends in Europe, with little left to distinguish us from any place else. We can experience the same averageness as the rest of the world—or you can join me, and we can fight for American exceptionalism.

Ancient scripture instructs us to adjust course when we see danger coming (Proverbs 27:12). In other words, when we see a problem ahead, we are to do something about it before it's too late. For now, we can still avert an irreversible disaster, but avoiding this manmade calamity will not happen by accident. There is a clear and distinct destination up ahead, and it is a place where most of us don't want to go. Now is the time to leave a legacy of liberty to our children.

My writing may strike some as alarmist. This would be out of character for me, as I'm an eternal optimist, and have even written a book on positive thinking called *The 4:8 Principle*. But staying positive doesn't mean remaining passive. Staying positive demands that you take productive action to solve or minimize the problems and predicaments in your life rather than simply hoping they will go away on their own. And the War on Success will not disappear spontaneously. We have to take action to stop it.

To be clear, I remain optimistic about the future of America—not because I believe in really big government, but because I believe in the really big God who inspires our nation. And, at risk of offending any of my polytheistic readers, I also have faith that this one and only Creator, who influenced our Founding Fathers, is still fully engaged and hungry to continue blessing our nation in exciting ways.

Furthermore, I believe in the potential of each and every American citizen. Our country will remain great as long as individual greatness is promoted, nurtured, and rewarded. This is not the case right now, but it can be again—if enough Americans stand up and insist on it. Remind yourself that over 58 million citizens voted against the direction in which we are heading. A single election does not discredit our heritage. We may be at the mercy of the statists temporarily, but our future is in our own hands.

Now is the time to mobilize!

PRINCIPLES MATTER MOST

The War on Success is a symptom of how far our nation has drifted from the Founders' formula for individual liberty and self-determination. There are other related signs, like the government's soaring deficit, excessive spending, and its habit of rewarding irresponsible behavior. We have, without much of a fight, allowed massive federal programs, and the second-rate government mindset that accompanies them, to invade our lives and infect our national attitude.

In other areas of life, we are fortunate to have symptoms that alert us to an impending problem or crisis. For example, signs of a heart attack include chest pain, shortness of breath, dizziness, and anxiety. In this scenario, though, it would be beneficial to recognize the early warning signs or contributing factors, such as excessive body fat, high cholesterol, insufficient exercise, and family history. If you monitored the advanced signs, you could spot danger ahead while there was still time to correct the situation.

Athletics provides another useful analogy. Sports are a great platform for teaching the lessons of life. As we know, the principles or fundamentals of each sport are often referred to as "the basics." In baseball, football, or lacrosse, the team that adheres to the fundamentals most consistently wins most consistently. This is how American life works as well, at least so far. It's really no mystery at all. In baseball, when a team drifts into a slump, it's often described as playing "sloppy ball." This simply means they have strayed from the fundamentals of winning baseball. Even a talent-packed team of superstars will stop winning consistently when it fails to execute the proper fundamentals. By refocusing on the basics, individuals, teams, and yes, even nations can break out of slumps.

The founding principles of liberty include limited government, strong property rights, governmental checks and balances, free markets, debt avoidance, and equal rights, not equal things. For individual citizens, these standards are translated into the expectation of self-reliance, personal initiative, individual responsibility, and resourcefulness. Recognizing the principles cultivated by our Founding Fathers illuminates our understanding and preserves the attitude of freedom.

One of the great red herrings of our time is the notion that complex problems require complex solutions—not only complex, but expensive and sophisticated, something that only the elite minds in D.C. can sufficiently comprehend. Certainly, some problems are more intricate than others, but it is the statist, not the entrepreneur, whose reputation has been built on turning a mole hill into a mountain range. The truth, however, is always simple. It always has been and always will be. It's hardly ever easy, but it's definitely simple.

I believe in the Principle of Parsimony, which states that we should keep explanations as succinct and simple as possible. Beware the leader who perpetuates the notion that solutions must be intricate. Follow basic principles, and life becomes very simple. Follow fads, and life becomes very complicated. This is true for an individual as well as a nation. The quick way into a mess is to violate timeless principles. The quickest way out of a mess is to reorient yourself in a manner consistent with principles. This is the inconvenient truth.

Predictably, the statist will insist that the Founders' principles are now obsolete. Many of these same state-loving folks dismiss the Bible as being antiquated and irrelevant as well. However, the Founders were highly educated students of history, philosophy, and the Bible. They distilled their knowledge into a brilliant Constitution that codified the workings of the entire American government in about ten pages (even including the first ten amendments that form the Bill of Rights). Compare this to the near 2,000-page healthcare reform proposal that passed the House of Representatives. Take a guess which document—the Constitution or the healthcare reform proposal—reflects clearer principles, more logical thinking, and will work better in practice.

The Founders wrote the Constitution to restrain the

THE STATIST'S PRAYER

Our Government who art in D.C.,
Hallowed be thy name,
Thy big programs come,
Thy will be done,
In every home as you dictate from Washington
Give us today what you believe we need and
Forgive us our debts
As we refuse to pay them
And lead us not into hard work,
But deliver us from Capitalism,
For thine is the ingenuity, wealth, and power for all of America forever and forever.
Amen!

nature of man, namely future government leaders. George Washington painted a clear picture of the hazards of political excess when he said, "Government is not reason, it is not eloquence—it is force. Like fire, it is a dangerous servant and a fearful master."[7] The Founders knew from the Bible that human nature cannot be changed, and they knew from history the perils of believing otherwise. Therefore, they exercised great caution when allocating to man authority over others. Recognizing the inherent downside of human nature, the Founders formulated a system of principles in which both the government and the citizens would be accountable to law. As Thomas Jefferson wrote, "Let no more be said of confidence in man, but bind him down from mischief by the chains of the Constitution."[8]

As an advisor and coach to more than a thousand entrepreneurs and their families, I've observed that when we stray from timeless principles, trouble and adversity are never far behind. There are unwavering principles that preside over each area of our lives as well as principles that govern our lives as a whole. When we attempt to bend, stretch, or otherwise pervert these principles, we set ourselves up for pain and regret. History's most successful individuals have resisted the natural human tendency to make up their own little "pet laws" of life and then rationalize their disillusionment when the inevitable fallout materializes. And as a nation, the further we've moved away from the Founders' principles, the bigger the mess we've gotten into.

Our constitutional system was designed to severely limit the government's power to meddle in the affairs of individuals. The founding principles were inspired from natural law or God's law.[9] For example, the natural law of "Thou Shall Not Steal" translates into the natural right of private property and ownership. The natural law of free will translates into the natural right of individual liberty. The natural law of sowing and reaping translates into the natural right of freedom to acquire through personal initiative.

These principles are as valid today as ever. How we apply them must surely change, but principles don't have expiration dates. No matter how often we abandon or slander them, they will still welcome us back like the prodigal son with open arms. We will, naturally, experience the repercussions of getting off track, but the right course is only a few principles away. Imagine your own child or another loved one deeply lost in her life. Imagine learning that your previously "successful" or "together" daughter was out of a job, deep in debt, on the brink of divorce, and had a substance addiction. Would you think, "Why bother, she's so lost, there's no hope," or "She's so far gone, we can only help her cope with the mess, not solve it"? Of course not. You would love her, encourage her, and help her get back to the basics in her own life. You'd fight for her future.

We're all capable of getting into a real mess. None of us are indestructible, and that goes for our country as well. What matters is not how far off track we are, but what we do next, and whether we can rediscover our fundamental principles.

It's important to note how President Obama uses the word "principle" as a synonym for "idea" or "theory." He frequently refers to his political goals—affordable health coverage, well-paying jobs, supporting Medicare, close regulation of business, redistributive justice—as "principles." As we know, these are not principles, but concepts.

A principle, however, is much more than a mere thought or presumption. It is an irrefutable truth, rooted in natural law, that has a history of producing predictable results. We must avoid confusing theory with principle. And when we return to our real principles—the Founders' principles—we're all going to feel a sense of tranquility and relief, like we've finally arrived back home after a long trip through the wilderness.

The War on Success is an imminent threat, but it can and must be countered and defeated. This book will show you how to do it.

CHAPTER TWO

AMERICA IS THE GREATEST COUNTRY EVER!

"America is a vast conspiracy to make you happy."
—JOHN UPDIKE

BEFORE WE FURTHER DISCUSS the War on Success, it's worth considering what makes America so special. After all, one might ask, would it really be so bad if America became like most other countries? If Americans are different from everyone else, isn't it possible that they're right and we're wrong?

I think a lot about those kinds of questions, and sometimes I get asked them. I've found that it doesn't take much to give people a little perspective on the issue. Once, after a group of clients began complaining about all the supposed problems in America, I asked them, "If America is not the greatest nation that exists, then which nation is? And why aren't you living there?"

No one volunteered an answer.

There's a reason why immigrants have streamed into America for over two hundred years: it's the greatest land of opportunity ever created. No matter where you come from, this is where you have a legitimate shot at designing your life and making your dreams come true. In America, your life can become an example for others to follow or a warning for others to heed. You can be born poor and earn a fortune, and you can be born rich and lose it all. Or you can create something for you and your family in the middle—it's up to you. What a country! You don't even have to be born here to think of yourself and be viewed by others as a true American. Unlike other countries where birth and ancestry determine citizenship, in America it's about taking ownership of the American ideals, culture, and way of life.

I risk being labeled as arrogant, since American patriotism seems to have gone out of fashion in certain intellectual circles. But I'll say it straight: America is the best of the best. And just in case you have any lingering doubts left over from college or from the last campaign season, let me back it up with four substantive arguments.

1. OUR CHARACTER

America's Judeo-Christian roots infuse our founding documents and form our country's greatest asset. Our collective character still carries the legacy of the godly men who boldly fought for our independence from England and established our republic. From the moral laws provided by the Ten Commandments to the inalienable rights bestowed upon us by our Creator, the Founders rightly considered strong religious beliefs to be a precondition to rock-solid character. "In God we trust," an expression first added to U.S. coins during the Civil War, is no mere political slogan, but rather an unshakable conviction upon which both the moral fiber of an individual and a nation must rest.

Individually, good character exists within each one of us to the degree that habits of virtue dominate habits of vice. More than any other single factor, our character is responsible for our achievement or underachievement in life. As any good football coach reminds his players, "Character is what you're made of." In politics, in business, in marriage, or in sports, "character," as Heraclitus put it, "is destiny." Likewise, the character of a nation is the sum total of its virtuous citizens. America's character is America's backbone.

America's distinctive character flows both from the Founding Fathers and the Heavenly Father who inspired them. Because of the moral legacy of our forefathers, and despite our imperfections, from its founding through this day America has demonstrated exceptional moral strength. As with individuals, a country's character is revealed when it is under fire. When an individual or a country is tested, you find out "what they're really made of." Time and time again, when America has been tested, the red, white, and blue fibers of virtue have been crisply and proudly illuminated.

For example, Todd Beamer, Jeremy Glick, and the other heroes of United Flight 93 revealed their character, and by extension the nation's character, when they were unexpectedly drafted into battle on the morning of September 11, 2001. Aware of the fate of the other hijacked planes, these martyrs counterattacked against the Islamic terrorists who intended to use their jetliner as a weapon to kill hundreds or perhaps thousands more Americans. Had these everyday American passengers lacked the courage of character to fight back, either the White House or the Capitol would probably have been destroyed. The bold sacrifice of the Flight 93 heroes is a great reminder of the role that individual citizens play in the defense of our freedoms. We have walked our talk better than any nation on earth.

Beginning with the bravery of our Founders and their fight for freedom, through numerous wars, the Great Depression, and the attacks of September 11, we have bounced back from adversity. And we have what it takes to make another comeback.

2. OUR PERSONALITY

Like her character, America's collective personality is incomparable. As a nation, we are an original masterpiece, a true work of art in progress. We take pride in our uniqueness and our independent way of thinking. We have faith in God and high expectations for ourselves. We are patriotic, never forgetting the enormous sacrifices that were made on our behalf. As Americans, we are kindhearted, generous, innovative, driven, fun-loving, forgiving, optimistic, honorable, and determined. We believe we are defined by these strengths and not by our weaknesses.

We also love a lot of different things beyond our freedom, such as baseball, hot dogs, and apple pie, of course, but also college football Saturdays and Superbowl Sundays, backyard barbeques on the Fourth of July and New Year's Eve in Times Square, F-150s and F-18s, Disneyland and Broadway, national parks and action movies, rally caps and come-from-behind wins, cowboy boots and country music, Olympic gold and Augusta green, NASCAR and fast cars, self-help and Starbucks, Superman and the Star Spangled Banner.

America undoubtedly has produced more famous people than any other country. Our national heroes are professional athletes and movie stars, but they're also inventors like Thomas Edison and Alexander Graham Bell, explorers like Lewis and Clark, and businessmen like Andrew Carnegie, as well as everyday people who did extraordinary deeds, like Rosa Parks and Todd Beamer.

We're proud of our famous sons and daughters, but it's regular Americans who define our unique national persona. Every day, millions of citizens from countless backgrounds chase their own adaptation of the American Dream.

Despite the fashionable anti-Americanism that dominates the European elite, America radiates a current of energy that attracts freedom-seeking individuals from around the globe. The electric blend of American personalities is palpable throughout the country. And when the gates of America are open (and even when they're closed), people always run in and not out.

3. OUR FREE MARKET

In America, anyone can make it and anyone can lose it. Capitalism is for everyone. The free market allows individuals to flourish. It allows opportunity, but it does not mandate results.

America provides more opportunity for more people to realize their dreams than any other country in history. The United States was designed for the common man with a dream, as opposed to the already rich and powerful. The systems of law and commerce were set up to reward self-reliance, entrepreneurship, and individual responsibility.

America is the platform that allows and encourages the average to become exceptional. There is no other place on the planet that is designed to help industrious people get more of what they want in life. Consequently, the opportunity for economic success here is unmatched.

But it is just that—an opportunity, not an entitlement. The concept of a free market is quite simple. It does not involve compulsion or coercion. Each individual has the right to enter the market and sell his goods or services for whatever amount other people are willing to pay. No one is forced to buy, and no one is forced to sell. To get the things we want in life, we create something that others want and then sell it to them at a price that makes them want to buy it. This model is based on cooperation and voluntary exchange.

People trade their money for a product or service because they believe they will be better off with the product than with the money they used to buy it. And the seller believes he'll be better off with the profit than with the product he sold. Both parties expect to be in a better position after the trade. These elementary free-market concepts have always been America's primary economic principles. We take our talents, skills, and other assets to the market and sell them for as much as someone else is willing to pay for them.

The free market has turned America into an incomparably prosperous country—no other large country even comes close to our per capita wealth. Still, critics decry our "inequality" and the plight of poor Americans. And there's no doubt that some Americans are struggling and that society needs a safety net for them. But our critics tend not to mention that even the poor have it far better in America than virtually anywhere else. According to Robert E. Rector of the Heritage Foundation,

HOW TO DIMINISH THE GREATEST NATION EVER...IN ONE GENERATION!

1. Take God out of public life, especially schools; it's produced such great results so far.

2. Discourage any citizen from rising above the crowd, for it certainly displays arrogance.

3. Make "success" a dirty word synonymous with selfishness and greed.

4. Celebrate mutual or societal responsibility and minimize personal responsibility.

5. Stop teaching patriotic history. Instead, emphasize our mistakes and portray our ancestors as ignorant savages.

6. Smother dissenting thought through intimidation and accusations of racism and bigotry.

7. Promote multiple everything—languages, cultures, values, and beliefs.

8. Rename un-American values to sound virtuous. For example, "moral equivalency" becomes "tolerance."

9. Elect as president someone without any business, military, or other practical experience. For example, find a "community organizer."

10. Entangle entrepreneurs and other risk takers with lots of regulations devised by non-risk takers.

Overall, the typical American defined as poor by the government has a car, air conditioning, a refrigerator, a stove, a clothes washer and dryer, and a microwave. He has two color televisions, cable or satellite TV reception, a VCR or DVD player, and a stereo. He is able to obtain medical care. His home is in good repair and is not overcrowded. By his own report, his family is not hungry, and he had sufficient funds in the past year to meet his family's essential needs.[1]

"Poor" American citizens also enjoy more living space than "average" citizens living in European cities such as Paris, London, Vienna, and Athens.[2] And let's be honest—in a world where nearly a billion people go hungry every day, you probably can't name another country where one of the biggest health problems among the poor is *obesity*.

Dinesh D'Souza, in his bestseller *What's So Great About America*, gives us his perspective as an immigrant from India, reminding us of some of the wonders of everyday American life that we native-born Americans tend to take for granted:

In America, the immigrant immediately recognizes that things are different. The newcomer who sees America for the first time typically experiences emotions that alternate between wonder and delight. Here is a country where everything works: The roads are clean and paper-smooth; the highway signs are clear and accurate; the public toilets function properly; when you pick up the telephone, you get a dial tone; you can even buy things from the store and then take them back. For the Third World visitor, the American supermarket is a thing to behold: endless aisles of every imaginable product, fifty different types of cereal, and multiple flavors of ice cream. The place is full of countless unappreciated inventions: quilted toilet paper, fabric softener, cordless telephones, disposable diapers, roll-on luggage, and deodorant. Some countries, even today, lack these conveniences.[3]

It is interesting to contrast the pro-American enthusiasm so common in immigrants with the weary dissatisfaction voiced by American "intellectuals" and other elite groups. It should be noted, however, that much of this discontent is exaggerated by the media. In fact, research shows that everyday Americans are really quite happy; a survey by Lake Research Partners during the peak of the economic crisis in late 2008 found that only 19 percent of American workers feel they are being excluded from the American Dream.[4] Similarly, a 2007 Harris Poll reported that 94 percent of Americans consider themselves either "satisfied" or "very satisfied" with their lives.[5]

The free market is inextricably linked to our quality of life. Ever wondered why a wildly disproportionate amount of the technological progress of the last hundred years has happened in the United States? It's because the free market encourages risk-taking, reward-achieving, creative breakthroughs, and scientific exploration. According to the Boston Consulting Group and *Business-Week*, sixteen of the twenty-five most innovative companies in the world are right here in the United States.[6] Is this dumb luck? Have Americans won a planetary lottery? Of course not! We are blessed indeed, but our success is no accident: progress and excellence thrive in a free market.

In *Capitalism: The Unknown Ideal*, Ayn Rand rightly praised the entrepreneurial class that has become the whipping boy of our current administration:

> Businessmen are the one group that distinguishes capitalism and the American way of life from the totalitarian statism that is swallowing the rest of the world. All the other social groups— workers, farmers, professional men, scientists, soldiers—exist

under dictatorships, even though they exist in chains, in terror, in misery, and in progressive self-destruction. But there is no such group as businessmen under a dictatorship. Their place is taken by armed thugs: by bureaucrats and commissars. Businessmen are the symbol of a free society—the symbol of America.[7]

The free market is certainly not perfect, and few would argue otherwise. But it has proven itself to be far better at creating more wealth for more people than any statist economy.

4. OUR GENEROSITY

America is the most generous nation in the world. In fact, no other country comes close to our combined private and government charity.

In 2007, American religious congregations gave $8.6 billion to the developing world. Congregations, foundations, corporations, and colleges and universities contributed a combined $36.9 billion, which is over one and a half times U.S. government aid for that same time period.[8]

Our government, via our tax dollars, has been the largest contributor to the United Nations every year since its creation in 1945. The United States contributed 41.5 percent, or $1.2 billion, of the 2006 budget of the World Food Program, which provides more than four million tons of food to nearly 100 million people throughout the world each year.[9] Under President George W. Bush, the United States provided $1.2 billion to combat malaria in Rwanda. Between 2003 and 2008, America prevented an estimated 1 million women from passing HIV to their babies, funded care for 3 million AIDS orphans, and provided medicine for more than 1.4 million AIDS victims.[10]

American individuals are also very generous. In 2006 alone, Americans donated about $295 billion to charitable causes. In the last fifty years, as GDP per person has risen almost 150 percent, charitable giving has increased 190 percent. The average American family gives more than $1,000 each year, with about two-thirds going to secular causes and one third going to religious institutions. And according to a 1995 study, we give, per capita, three and a half times as much to charities as the French, seven times more than the Germans, and fourteen times more than the Italians. Interestingly, in 2000, religious people gave four times more than secularists and volunteered twice as much; in fact, the religious folks even exceeded their secular counterparts in giving to nonreligious causes. What's more, in one survey, self-described "conservatives" gave 30 percent more to charity than self-described "liberals," even though the liberals earned 6 percent more per year.[11]

What can we learn from this brief survey of American greatness? First and foremost, America is an exceptional country. It is different from all others because the people are different—our national character was shaped by our unique values and by the circumstances of our nation's founding through our fight for liberty. We have nothing against other nations, but we have our own destiny. We're something special. As F. Scott Fitzgerald wrote, "France was a land, England a people, but America, having about it still that quality of idea, was harder to utter."[12]

America has its share of critics, both inside and outside our borders. And when you compare America to a utopian fantasy, we don't fare so well. But remember this: neither does any other country, especially those that have tried to fabricate government-driven prosperity. When you get a dose of reality and compare us to the rest of the world, you see that Dorothy was right: there really is "no place like home."

We have a unique country, a distinct national character, and an unmatched way of life. And that's worth fighting for.

CHAPTER THREE

TROPHIES
FOR EVERYONE

*"If we all did the things we are capable of doing, we could
literally astound ourselves."*

—THOMAS EDISON

Now THAT WE'VE DECIDED that success is worth fighting for, let's study the enemy of success in a bit more detail in order to improve our battle plan.

The War on Success is the primary tactic the Obama administration is using to advance statism. It relies on the spread of five state-sponsored attitudes that taint citizens and politicians alike and spread mediocrity throughout the country. These toxic attitudes are, in the long run, much more dangerous to our nation's health than the "toxic assets" that have lately generated so much media hype. I've nicknamed these state-sponsored attitudes "statitudes" because they represent the crooked thinking patterns that breed excessive government.

Have you ever thought much about your attitude? Our attitude is simply the way in which we habitually think. It is the lens or filter through which we process what's happening in the world. Statitudes, in contrast, are perspectives on life promoted by the state. They are mental blocks to individual success that are fed to the ignorant and apathetic. These statist mindsets invite dependence on the state, not oneself, on government, not God. With the complicity of a supine, left-leaning media, these toxic attitudes have been spreading for some time. And with the Obama administration they have been turbo-boosted with a stiff dose of statist steroids.

Stimulating the progressive "dumbing down" of America, statitudes have gradually eroded the self-reliant, industrious, and resourceful mindset that spurred America's greatness in the first place. We've allowed these noxious attitudes to seep into our psyche and reshape how we see ourselves and the world. We've lost our wisdom, our character, and our sense of destiny in the world at large. Like an old-fashioned convoy of ships, we've slowed down mentally to accommodate the slowest vessel.

Statitudes distill basic moral precepts into a fog of feel-good relativism. The purpose is to eliminate the concept of absolute truth so that our most basic values and morals become inverted. The productive, not the unproductive, are labeled as society's problem. The irresponsible, not the responsible, are rewarded. We're told that spending helps us get out of debt. We take one person's earnings, hand it to someone else, and call it "justice." We worship the earth but not its creator. We blame guns for killing, society for the addict, and the rich for the poor. We extol "diversity" and "tolerance," but vilify politically incorrect speech. We suppress excellence, achievement, and individual virtue, but celebrate mediocrity, stupidity, and perversion.

And of course, most crucially, the successful are demonized as oppressors, while the unsuccessful are exalted as noble victims of a heartless society.

As my friend and the author of *30 Ways in 30 Days to Save Your Family*, Rebecca Hagelin, says, "We live in a culture that has gone stark raving mad." Unfortunately, this is not even a slight exaggeration.

In the next few chapters, I will describe the five statitudes that many Americans, possibly a voting majority, have come to accept as true, right, and even noble, when in fact they subvert the individualistic American character and foster government dependence. My arguments here may strike some as callous, but there's no value in soft-pedaling the threat these statitudes present to our liberty and opportunity. These obstructive attitudes should be discussed candidly so every citizen can recognize them and then neutralize them as necessary. Those who knowingly or unknowingly adopt these attitudes will sacrifice their shot at the American Dream, instead setting themselves up for frustration, averageness, and a lifetime of dependence. And even those who resist them will suffer as these statitudes spread through society, bringing down the competitiveness, innovation, and entrepreneurship that have always defined the American way.

THE FAIRNESS STATITUDE

Life is not fair.

We all learned when we were kids that fairness is when everybody plays by the same rules. In a neighborhood game of pickup baseball, for example, teams agree ahead of time where the foul lines will be, what constitutes a homerun, and any other modifications of standard rules. The same rules then apply to both teams. Likewise, in a track meet, all runners use the same starting line and finish line. The same goes for a hot dog eating contest: everyone gets the same amount of time to eat as many hotdogs as they can. This is simple, straightforward, and common sense.

The opposite of fairness, though, is called "rigging" or "fixing." This is when the rules are manipulated to favor one individual or group over the others. To illustrate this, imagine that we want to rig a baseball game to give the blue team an advantage over the red team. What are some of the things we could do? We could start by making the homerun mark closer for the blue team. Then we could give each player on the blue team four strikes instead of three. Finally, we could choose an older sibling from one of the blue team's players as the umpire and suggest to him that any close calls should favor the blue team.

Mysteriously, this rigging or fixing is also labeled in many quarters as "fairness" and "equality." But how could this be true? How can the opposite of fairness also be called "fairness"? It's even spelled the same way. We all need to be aware of this intriguing word game. Fairness in this sense is wholly un-American!

We can all remember the bratty kid from our childhood who was always complaining that things were not fair. If he didn't finish his quiz on time, it wasn't fair because of the noise or the lighting, or he didn't feel well or some other bogus reason. If he lost any competition, he'd insist on a "do-over" or stomp off in a huff.

Make sure your kids know that real fairness is when everyone plays by the same rules, enforced by an impartial referee. Point out real life examples of both fairness and fixing. What ever happened to the clear-cut concept of fairness? Has it been lost in a gray sea of equality, subjectivity, and relativity?

For statists, above all else, things must be fair. And by "things," they mean everything. And by "fair," they don't mean equal opportunity or equal rules—they mean equal outcomes.

The problem is that life is naturally unfair. Liberty breeds inequality—when people are free, those who are smarter, better motivated, and harder-working will achieve more than others. So the only way to ensure equal outcomes is to strangle liberty. In other words, the more government tries to make life fair, the less fair it becomes.

Fairness is a pleasant-sounding word for sure, but it is no substitute for freedom. And when applied by the government, the fairness statitude depresses freedom by manipulating results in favor of a preferred individual or group. Thus, "fairness" has become standard code language for all sorts of social engineering objectives that clash with the intentions of our Founding Fathers, including but not limited to income redistribution, affirmative action, gender quotas, and minority set-asides. Just about the only "fair" thing a statist doesn't like is a fair tax.

In school, in sports, and in the free market, the rules should be fair so that anyone utilizing their talent, work ethic, and resourcefulness has the opportunity to succeed. For example, the punishment for stealing should be the same for the rich, the poor, the pretty, the ugly, the smart, the stupid, the kind, and the rude.

And we should expect that our individual rights are not sacrificed at the altar of some amorphous "greater good." We should have a level playing field, with the government acting as an impartial referee. Statists, however, claim a level playing field is impossible without constantly rigging the rules in favor of select groups. So in effect, a statist government is a referee that rejects impartiality from the beginning. "Fairness" used to be a progression toward an ideal, but it has become a regression toward tyranny.

"Fairness" does not appear in America's founding documents for good reason—it infuses the government with arbitrary power it was never intended to have. You may ask, "But what about the Founders' assertion in the Declaration of Independence that all men are created equal"? Well, let's look at the full sentence: "We hold these truths to be self-evident, that all men are created equal, that they are endowed by their Creator with certain unalienable rights, that among these are Life, Liberty, and the pursuit of Happiness." This means we are equal in God's eyes as human beings, equal as citizens in the eyes of the court, and will have our individual rights equally protected.

But the Founders never believed that all choices, all behaviors, and all talents are equal. They didn't think the thoughtful and industrious are equal to the thoughtless and lazy. John Adams emphasized this when he wrote,

> That all men are born to equal rights is true. Every being has a right to his own, as clear, as moral, as sacred, as any other being has. . . . But to teach that all men are born with equal powers and faculties, to equal influence in society, to equal property and advantages through life, is a gross fraud, as glaring an imposition on the credulity of the people, as ever was practiced by monks, by Druids, by Brahmins, by priests of the immortal Lama, or by the self-styled philosophers of the French Revolution.[1]

Equalization ignores the natural order of things. Wherever you look, you'll find that creation yields an inequitable distribution of resources and wealth. Florida has no mountains. Tennessee is ocean challenged. Arizona misses out on the Georgia humidity, and there are no deserts in Pennsylvania. Some countries have greater natural resources than others. While one country has preferable geography, another has a better climate. There is great variety throughout nature, and this is not something that can be "fixed" or "equalized."

Furthermore, our Creator saw fit to bestow personal assets such as talent, creativity, physical strength, physical appearance, intelligence, and other qualities on an unequal basis. This in itself creates inequality and unfairness. If you're five-foot-two and play in the NBA, you're going to have a very unfair experience. If you go into engineering but have difficulty with simple math, your career will seem quite unfair. If you're in sales but you don't like talking to strangers, your commission checks will reflect some serious inequality. If you possess my singing voice and expect to win *American Idol*, you are going to find the experience outrageously unfair.

After much reflection, I've decided to accept that Tiger Woods is a better golfer than I am. In fact, I admire him and wish him even greater success. I also hold no ill will toward other authors who have sold more books than I have. To the contrary, I applaud them, look up to them, and want to learn from them. I am even fine with my fellow Americans who are much younger than I am, but have a nicer second home than my only home. I have no resentment or animosity toward any of these people who are more "privileged" than I, as our president would say. Why would I? Why would I be resentful toward someone who has reached some of the goals that I myself would like to reach?

God loves us all equally, and this is why he created us all in His likeness, despite our individual differences. And, just maybe, God is more interested in our spiritual equity than our material equality.

Everybody has handicaps, weaknesses, or other crosses to bear. But a big part of the American experience is learning to overcome our disadvantages, or even transform them into advantages. This requires spiritual growth and the development of our character. If we want to perpetuate American exceptionalism, we have to get beyond this preoccupation with fairness and equality. Regardless of the circumstances of your birth, I say, "Grab a helmet, get off the sidelines, and get in the game!"

But too often today, those on the sidelines are establishing new ground rules for those of us who are actually in the game. As Democratic congressman Barney Frank boasted, "We are trying in every front to increase the role of government in the regulatory area." Clearly, the congressman doesn't realize that when politicians like him put reams of needless regulations on the rest of us, they are not making anything more equal or more fair—they're just creating barriers to opportunity for all Americans.

John Griffith, the famed coach and athletic director at Drake University in the early 1900s, put it all in perspective: "I do not want anybody to convince my son that someone will guarantee him a living. I want him rather to realize that there is plenty of opportunity in this country for him to achieve success. But whether he wins or loses depends entirely on his own character, his own perseverance, his own thrift, intelligence, capacity for hard work."

WE'RE ALL WINNERS...NOT!

Here's a line that drives me nuts. "You're all winners!" What the heck does this mean? Of course we're not all winners. But in our society, the truth has become unspeakable: some of us are losers. See, it's not that bad. I said it aloud. (Or wrote it.) I'm not kidding, either. How could we all be winners unless the definition of winning has been "statified" to include mere participation? By definition, we can't have winners unless we have losers.

Youth sports used to be a great venue to develop character through competition, as kids tasted both victory and defeat. But sports are being degraded as they're increasingly infected by the fairness statitude. Some youth leagues around the nation don't even keep score anymore—even though the kids themselves do—in an apparent attempt to neutralize the concept of winning and losing.

For several decades now, many youth leagues and coaches have tried to make things "fair" by awarding trophies to everyone just for playing on the team. We can think of this as "Early Onset Entitlement." To compound the dynamic, those who should be singled out for merit are overlooked, and those who don't deserve recognition receive it for just showing up.

Don't get the wrong impression. I am a big believer in and have taught courses on self-esteem and self-confidence for both adults and children for many years. But giving someone something he has not earned does not strengthen his self-worth or build

MAKING LIFE FAIR

Kurt Vonnegut's short story "Harrison Bergeron" offers a good sense of the wackiness of social leveling:

> THE YEAR WAS 2081, and everybody was finally equal. They weren't only equal before God and the law. They were equal every which way. Nobody was smarter than anybody else. Nobody was better looking than anybody else. Nobody was stronger or quicker than anybody else. All this equality was due to the 211th, 212th, and 213th Amendments to the Constitution, and to the unceasing vigilance of agents of the United States Handicapper General.[2]

In Vonnegut's tale, the main character Harrison was blessed with more intelligence than he needed, so he had to wear bulky headphones that emitted periodic sharp noises and a pair of spectacles with thick, wavy lenses. Together, these devices prevented him from taking unfair advantage of his brain. Since he also had above normal strength, scrap metal was hung upon him to weaken and tire him. And to offset his good looks, the H–G men required that he always wear a red rubber ball for a nose, keep his eyebrows shaved off, and cover some of his white teeth with black caps. As for the story's gorgeous and graceful ballerina, she had to wear a hideous mask to offset her beauty and a lug a bag of birdshot around her neck to diminish her dancing ability.

This got me thinking—it seems there's much more we could do to make things more equal.

ATTRACTIVENESS: We should manufacture both zit eruption cream and foul breath lozenges for those who are excessively attractive. And, for just the top 1 percent of really, really attractive people, we could also limit their personal hygiene habits. Don't worry; this will not affect folks of average attractiveness like most of us. As one's attractiveness may vary with the passage of time, we must set up a "good looks commission," possibly headed by Nancy Pelosi, to calibrate the level of handicapping. Any reclassification will involve the standard attractiveness transfer fee.

continued

continued

PERSONALITY: In order to give hope to the dull and unpleasant, we must moderate the unfair advantage that accompanies a charming personality and a good sense of humor. Possibly a standardized, web-based assessment could be administered to all citizens and results could be scored and evaluated by ACORN. Those who are deemed to have excessive charisma or who are just really fun people shall have their social activities curtailed. This type of charismatic intervention prevents citizens from having unacceptable influence within their demographic reference group and, more importantly, brings justice to those who have the misfortune of being jerks.

METABOLISM: We should develop a fat pill to slow down the metabolism of those who can unfairly stay skinny. For enforcement, weekly weigh-ins and body fat analyses could be conducted at government healthcare checkpoints, located adjacent to most postal centers. Alternatively, these people of metabolic privilege could be forced to eat a pint or more of Ben and Jerry's Hubby-Hubby ice cream nightly before bedtime.

CREATIVITY: Those who can unfairly generate really valuable ideas on a regular basis must be prohibited from thinking on certain days of the week. To monitor these thinking holidays, a special helmet could be worn that prevents independent thinking or life-enhancing thought of any kind. In lieu of thinking restrictions or the nuisance of the helmet, these creatively privileged individuals may opt instead for logging into the centralized idea database and sharing their ideas with the innovation czar who will disperse selected ideas for the common good.

HAIR: We must enforce monthly compulsory thinning treatments for the full-headed or excessive hair crowd, leaving at least one noticeable bald spot on their crown. Alternatively, these privileged citizens, who have more hair than they need, may use both the zit cream and the foul breath lozenges. As a follicly-challenged American, I have a vested interest in this one, but since we can't spread the hair around, we at least need to level the playing field a little.

anything desirable. While there is no harm in recognizing participation, a trophy should be reserved for accomplishment, excellence, and for demonstrated leadership skills. Its purpose is to
motivate not only the deserving recipient, but other ambitious athletes who aspire to get the next trophy.

Game balls—an old tradition in which the top performer in a
particular game is given an honorary game ball—work the same
way. They reward and inspire. Those are two great words when
you put them in the context of rewarding success and inspiring
greatness. But again, that's not how game balls are always used
anymore. I assisted a coach a few years ago who planned out in
advance when each player on his team would be given the game
ball. It was nice, I suppose, but by the third or fourth game, the
kids had caught on to the well-meaning ruse. I know of super-
markets and banks that follow the same program with grown-ups,
pre-determining the employee of the month a year ahead of time
to make sure no one gets overlooked. And the result is the same
as for the coach's game balls—an honor loses any meaning when
it's given out to everyone.

Besides, the "trophies for everyone" mentality does not reflect
how the real world works. It's building up kids' expectation of
getting something for nothing, and it's teaching that life rewards
participation, not results. It prepares kids to expect that life will
always be fair and that it's not particularly important how much
or how little they accomplish.

This is a good recipe for raising children who don't accomplish
much.

WE EARN THIS DISTINCTION

In America, we are not born a winner or a loser. We earn this distinction. Losing is not a permanent designation, nor is winning. I
know as many losers born into privilege as I do winners born into

humble circumstances. Americans appreciate this truth and, until recently, have tended to celebrate the successful.

What statists and other equality-mongers don't understand is that there is value in losing. I have been a loser far more than I have been a winner (no jokes, please), and every time I lose, it spurs me to work even harder so I don't have to be a loser again the next time around. If every competition had to finish in a tie, it would end competition and quickly become a bore to watch. Winning may not be everything, but it is right up there with oxygen. Are athletics the last, great hope of true freedom to excel? Or will they fall to the War on Success as well?

Hitting a baseball prepared me for the reality of American life—I got acclimated to succeeding (getting a hit) only 30 or 40 percent of the time. That prepared me for the inherent inequities of life, as did the pitchers who could throw the ball past me, my opponents who could outrun me, and so on.

I didn't miss a sinking curve ball and complain that it was unfair. Instead, I invested the time in the batting cage so I would be better prepared next time. Because of my work ethic, I surpassed many who had more natural talent. And some were better than me, and I accepted that. But I always strove to get better—I never strove for "equality." In fact, I believed in—and still believe in—*inequality*: striving to make yourself better than others through the development of wisdom and the persistent application of your talent bank.

We can make ourselves unequal by the way we lead our lives. Yes, we can. Earned inequality is a virtuous achievement to be celebrated.

Proponents of fairness and equalization believe they can reorganize society to make everything fair and equal for everyone. Unfortunately, this way of thinking has become entrenched in all levels of education and has reached epidemic proportions throughout our culture.

To save success, we must first learn to recognize these insidious attempts at social leveling. Listen for the buzz words. Whenever you hear someone speaking of equality and fairness, pause and mentally substitute the phrase "equal outcomes," because that is often their real goal. This means equal results, equal grades, and equal goodies. As President Lyndon Johnson foolishly said in a 1965 commencement address, "We seek not just freedom but opportunity. We seek not just legal equity but human ability, not just equality as a right and a theory but equality as a fact and equality as a result."[3]

Eric Hoffer explained the impulse driving this mania for equality:

> Those who see their lives as spoiled and wasted crave equality and fraternity more than they do freedom. If they clamor for freedom, it is but freedom to establish equality and uniformity. The passion for equality is partly a passion for anonymity: to be one thread of the many which make up a tunic; one thread not distinguishable from the others. No one can then point us out, measure us against others and expose our inferiority.[4]

We cannot make life fair. It is both impossible and undesirable. Anyone who loves equality more than freedom is likely to wind up with neither. Trying to manufacture equality is bad for individuals, since giving an advantage to "more deserving" individuals infringes on the rights of unprotected or "less deserving" citizens. And it's bad for the country, since we can't progress toward a colorblind society when we have different rules for people depending on their race, sex, or some other metric. To paraphrase the great Rodney King, "Can't we all just play by the same rules?"

To sum up: imagine the sound of a group of 5-year-olds playing together and whining that it's unfair that one kid has more than the others—maybe it's more toys or more candy or more games. For them, whining is okay. After all, they're only five. It might even be a little funny.

But when politicians with real power over our lives wail about fairness and use the force of government to try to achieve it, it's not so funny anymore.

THE VICTIMITIS STATITUDE

Few qualities today shout "mediocrity" more than the modern notion of victimhood. Victimhood is the group-based and activist-proclaimed state of helplessness and hopelessness that spreads like the swine flu from state to state throughout our great land. Charles Sykes, author of *A Nation of Victims*, points out, "If you add up all the groups that consider themselves to be victims or oppressed, their number adds up to almost 400 percent of the population."[5] For most of us, this perpetual gala of chronic victims is nothing less than exhausting.

This constitutes the next statitude that all patriots need to be aware of: *Victimitis*. It is the inflammation of the grievance gland which, if not treated rapidly with a dose of moral fiber, can permanently immobilize individuals and even entire groups.

This statitude is similar to a relationship in which one chronically dissatisfied partner tries to make the other person feel guilty as a way of manipulating their behavior for self-seeking gain. Despite the authenticity of his gripes with society, when a citizen thinks, speaks, and behaves as a victim, he shuts down all honest channels for securing a dignified life. Again, Eric Hoffer explains succinctly in *The Passionate State of Mind*, "There are many who find a good alibi far more attractive than an achievement. For an achievement does not settle anything permanently. We still have to prove our worth anew each day: we have to prove that we are as good today as we were yesterday. But when we have a valid

THE WOODS, ARMSTRONG, MANNING FAIRNESS ACT OF 2010

Whereas Tiger Woods has won an excessive number of PGA tour events compared with other professional golfers, and consequently has profited from disproportionate endorsement activities.

Whereas Lance Armstrong has won the Tour de France more than any other cyclist in history, displacing the potential success of other equally deserving racers.

Whereas the Manning family has exploited their genetic talent bank for athletic and economic gain in both the NCAA and the NFL, hurting the chances of success for other hard working players.

Whereas we have seen a marked decline in the self-esteem of other athletes when competing in sports with a dominant or recurring champion.

For the ideals of equalization and excellence for all, we hereby pronounce this Act of Athletic Justice.

From this day forward, the following persons will be excluded from participating in all competitions occurring within the United States:

1. An individual who has won the event in question in the previous five years.

2. An individual who has won five events of equal or lesser value in the last ten years.

3. An individual finishing in the top 10 of one or more events in the past year.

alibi for not achieving anything we are fixed, so to speak, for life."[6]

Of course there are true victims in any society. And despite the relentless hype, it's pretty easy to distinguish legitimate victims from the phonies. We see the wife and young children of the fallen police officer. We see the family losing everything to a tornado. We see the anguished parents returning home after burying their teenage son. We see the battered wife seeking shelter. We see the young boy fighting cancer. We see a young girl reaching for her toys from her wheelchair. We see nightly the victims of today's violent crime. And we still see, as though it were yesterday, the victims of the terrorist attacks of September 11, along with their families.

Most of us have firsthand experience of true victims and the hardships they endure. And if you have that experience, you've probably noticed that people who prematurely lose loved ones to disease or sudden death never recover or "get over it." But they learn to deal with it over time, and they refuse to let it define them as individuals. Ironically, true victims seldom choose to see themselves as victims at all, and their fellow Americans typically shower them with love, support, and generosity.

Victimitis, however, is completely different. Victimitis occurs when the victim label is permanently and proudly affixed to the heart and mind of an individual or to groups of individuals, in order to advance an agenda or win an advantage over others. Seeing themselves as permanently wronged, those suffering from Victimitis focus their energy on nursing old wounds or reliving the historical suffering of their group. In the blunt words of Dr. Phil McGraw, "These people are accountable for nothing. Everything is done to them, not by them or with them or for them. They see themselves as captives on the evil train of life, and all the other passengers are out to get them."[7] This prolonged basking in past wrongs, whether real or imagined, slowly rots a person's character despite any superficial gains that may be realized.

Legendary basketball coach John Wooden famously said, "Don't let what you cannot do interfere with what you can do." Permanent victims turn this sound advice on its head. They focus on the fact that they're not succeeding, rather than on how they could. With the enabling of their role models, mentors, and community leaders, they define themselves by their deficiencies and inadequacies. Consequently, their thinking gets conditioned by

UNLEASH THE VICTIM WITHIN!

Deep inside all of us is a delicate victim yearning to escape into the real world. To assist in this liberation, follow these seven steps.

1. *Affiliate with a proven victim group or any group that has been conferred special rights by the state.* While this is not essential to permanent victim status, it provides a good head start. The side benefit of hanging out with other like-minded victims is that you will effortlessly start acting more like them. You'll develop the thought patterns and daily habits that produce quality victims. Developing strong codependent relationships with other victims can also accelerate your own victimhood.

2. *Avoid taking ownership of your behavior.* You may have said something stupid or done something wrong or neglected the important things in life for years, but that doesn't mean you should have to face the consequences. What happens to you is outside your control. Know that your choices have been predetermined by your circumstances.

3. *Stay immobilized.* Nothing will get you out of victim status faster than doing something productive to improve your situation. To overcome this urge to take charge of your life, start thinking about all the things you can't do, the mistakes you've made, and how far behind you are. Meditate upon your disappointments and dissatisfactions. This will keep you rightly discouraged and will help you procrastinate more effectively. Many victims find it helpful to keep a picture or other image that reminds them of injustice and evokes resentment of some kind. Possibly visualize an evil capitalist.

4. *Master VictimSpeak.* The words you use shape your thinking. Avoid phrases that suggest confidence like "I can do it," "I'll get it done," or "You can count on me." Instead say things like "It's no use," "Why bother," "I don't feel like it," "I can't," or "It's not my fault." Tell yourself and others that your situation will no doubt deteriorate. Come up with your own personalized, disempowering phrases and work them into as many conversations as possible.

continued

continued

5. ***Assume the worst about the future.*** Affirm that the future is likely to be just like the past and probably worse. Do what you can, or as little as you can, to ensure your prediction comes true. Keep your chin down so you won't miss any new opportunities for being disadvantaged or oppressed. Refuse to entertain the notion that others have been where you are and have overcome their adversity. This is nothing but mean-spirited, self-reliant propaganda.

6. ***Become a spokesperson for the cause.*** Hitch your wagon to something larger than yourself. Exploit opportunities for media exposure with alternating bouts of crying and outbursts of indignant anger. Use dramatic words when the camera is rolling like, "outraged," "shocked," "horrible," and "devastated." These make great sound bites that can be replayed often. Reaffirm your victim status publicly as much as possible.

7. ***Stay the course.*** As obstacles will certainly come, don't bother resisting; let them overtake you. The path to permanent victimhood can be very rewarding and liberating. The small price you have to pay today can turn into small reward down the road. And with very little work on your part, you can become the type of victim that other victims admire.

what they can't do rather than what they could do. This learned helplessness is a prescription for a lesser life, not because one is a victim, but because he has chosen "victim" as his primary identity.

The goal of those infected with Victimitis is to evade both the responsibility and the corresponding consequences of their choices. Dr. Ofer Zur describes this phenomenon:

> In claiming the status of victim and by assigning all blame to others, a person can achieve moral superiority while simultane-

ously disowning any responsibility for one's behavior and its outcome. The victims "merely" seek justice and fairness. If they become violent, it is only as a last resort, in self-defense. The victim stance is a powerful one. The victim is always morally right, neither responsible nor accountable, and forever entitled to sympathy.[8]

None of us would want this life for our children, and as a culture we should make it a priority to focus on future potential rather than past grievances. As Thomas Jefferson reflected, "I like the dreams of the future better than the history of the past."[9]

We Americans are the most compassionate people in the world. We take care of ourselves (which is a very compassionate thing to do), and we take care of our families, our friends, and our neighbors. We love to help others, especially when they are in need.

But with an elite political culture in power, the hunt for fresh victims to pander to is well underway. With every complaint comes another opportunity to "fix the injustice" by inflating government and intruding on the personal freedom of everyone else. The victim industry even stays strong when the economy is weak.

But when an individual sees himself as a chronic victim, he can only be helped temporarily. Former NFL standout Burgess Owens said, "I don't look at an obstacle as something that somebody's doing against me. I look at it as an opportunity to gain some character, to learn a great lesson of life, so I can turn back one day and tell somebody, 'You know what? I made it through that—you can do the same thing.'"[10]

We cannot both reinforce victimhood and create victors. We have to make a choice between the two. And so the statist does no favors by making excuses for self-destructive choices and counterproductive behavior. We should never sanctify victimhood. Instead of enabling great victims with their list of grievances, government should empower great citizens with lists of possibilities.

Politicians need not be in the business of pandering to permanent victims.

Unfortunately, Barack Obama is a deep believer in Victimitis. You'd think someone's election as President of the United States would be enough to wash away the victim mentality, but that's not so. Not only does Obama still passionately cling to victimhood, he actively tries to spread the grievance culture among Americans. On the campaign trail, here's what he told a group of American Indian tribal leaders:

> I was growing up in Hawaii at the time and where I was grow
> ing up, there weren't a lot of black families, and so sometimes I
> was looked at as sort of an outsider and so I know what it's like
> to be on the outside.... I know what it's like to not always have
> been respected or to have been ignored and I know what it's like
> to struggle and that's how I think many of you understand
> what's happened here on the reservation, that a lot of times you
> have been forgotten just like African-Americans have been for
> gotten or other groups in this country have been forgotten and
> because I have that experience.[11]

It seems to me that the biggest threat we face is not global warming, it's global whining. Barack Obama went to Columbia and Harvard Law School and was elected to the Senate and then to the presidency. Who exactly "ignored" him? How has he been "forgotten"? And why is this exceptional man identifying with and nurturing victimhood instead of using himself as an example of the boundless opportunities America offers to everyone who shows initiative?

Victimitis is a debilitating condition that should be stamped out, not spread at the highest level of our government. It's a crucial part of the War on Success that needs to be recognized, resisted, and routed.

CHAPTER FOUR

ENVY: THE *REAL* OPIATE OF THE MASSES

"Envy is the most stupid of vices, for there is no single advantage to be gained from it."

—HONORÉ DE BALZAC

TURNING CITIZENS AGAINST EACH OTHER is a crucial part of the War on Success. And no tool is better at sowing that kind of social strife than our next statitude—*envy*. Immensely powerful, envy can make an individual absolutely miserable, and it can rapidly divide and disrupt a civil society. Forbidden by the Ten Commandments and also one the Seven Deadly Sins, envy is when we feel resentful because someone else has attained what we want. This could be a material possession or a position in life. It could be power, talent, good looks, or social standing. Not only do the envious begrudge what others have, they wish the other person to be deprived of it. This is an insidious emotion that brings out the basest instincts in human nature.

A lot has been written about envy through the ages. The Old Testament teaches, "Envy and wrath shorten the life."[1] Likewise, an old English proverb warns that "envy shoots at others, but wounds herself." In Dante's "Purgatory," the envious are punished by having their eyelids sewn shut because they enjoyed seeing others diminished. And Socrates had quite strong feelings on the topic, commenting, "Envy is the daughter of pride, the author of murder and revenge, the begetter of secret sedition, the perpetual tormenter of virtue. Envy is the filthy slime of the soul; a venom, a poison, a quicksilver, which consumeth the flesh and drieth up the bones."[2]

Envy eats up individuals, and class envy weakens nations. President Reagan once asked, "Since when do we in America believe that our society is made up of two diametrically opposed classes—one rich, one poor—both in a permanent state of conflict and neither able to get ahead except at the expense of the other? Since when do we in America accept this alien and discredited theory of social and class warfare? Since when do we in America endorse the politics of envy and division?"[3]

Although Reagan took a public stance against envy, our current president has a different attitude. Obama *stokes* envy, especially class envy. He spreads it and stews in it. In Obama's eyes, America is divided between the evil rich and the virtuous exploited, and the only solution is to take from the former group and give to the latter. In fact, Obama demonizes not only the "rich," but the very act of engaging in business and making money. For him, financial success is a dishonorable goal—perversely, money is something to be taken from others, not to be earned for oneself. As he told graduating students at a commencement ceremony at Southern New Hampshire University,

> In a few minutes, you can take your diploma, walk off this stage, and go chasing after the big house and the large salary and the nice suits and all the other things that our money culture says you should buy. But I hope you don't. Focusing your life solely on making a buck shows a poverty of ambition. It asks too little of yourself. And it will leave you unfulfilled.[4]

I've worked with thousands of entrepreneurs over the last twenty years, and I've yet to run into a single individual "focusing solely on making a buck." I'm sure they're out there, but you'd think I would have bumped into at least one by now.

Here are some important questions for the president: "What is your problem with what we earn? And why is it your business to judge whether what we have is 'excessive?'"

First Lady Michelle Obama is even blunter than her husband, admonishing a group of Ohio women,

> Don't go into corporate America. You know, become teachers. Work for the community. Be social workers. Be a nurse. Those are the careers that we need, and we're encouraging our young people to do that. But if you make that choice, as we did, to move out of the money-making industry into the helping industry, then your salaries respond.[5]

Anti-business resentment and class envy infuse the Obamas' speeches. Consider their careful choice of words—"chasing after the big house and the large salary and the nice suits," "focusing solely on making a buck shows a poverty of ambition," and "move out of the money-making industry into the helping industry." Wow, I didn't realize all those people with nice suits and big houses didn't help anyone. I always thought they created a lot more jobs than community organizers do, paid a lot more taxes, and donated a lot more to charity to boot.

These themes, which the Obamas repeat in speech after speech, reveal a poverty of understanding about capitalism and about the myriad ways society benefits when individuals succeed.

By the way, in light of Michelle's jeremiad against the "money-making industry," let's look at a snapshot of the Obamas' financial picture. Michelle's salary in 2004 was $122,000 and nearly tripled by 2005 to $317,000.⁶ Barack's income jumped from $207,647 in 2004 to $1,655,106 in 2005, then an off year of just $983,826 in 2006, then $4,200,000 in 2007, and $2,656,902 in 2008.⁷ During this time period, the president's charitable giving averaged 4.8 percent of his adjusted gross income.

Whatever the "money-making industry" is, the Obamas have certainly found it! And so has Barack's Chief of Staff, Rahm Emanuel, who earned more than $16 million in two and a half years as an investment banker.⁸ And so has Obama's National Economic Council director, Lawrence Summers, who earned $5.2 million in 2008 working for a hedge fund management company.⁹ And the list goes on.

But I'm happy for their wealth. I think it's great that the Obamas and their operatives have done so well financially. I just don't like their hypocritical condemnation of the rest of us.

Nearly all statists share these feelings of envy and resentment of the successful. Here are a few examples:

- Hillary Clinton: "Many of you are well enough off.... We're going to take things away from you on behalf of the common good."[10]
- Robert Reich: "Tax the Wealthy to Keep Everyone Healthy."[11]
- Joe Biden: "They [the middle class] deserve the tax breaks, not the wealthy who are doing well."[12]
- Richard Gephardt: "Those who have prospered and profited from life's lottery have a moral obligation to share their good fortune."[13]

The president and his allies seldom speak publicly without blaming something on either the rich or on capitalism in general. While their comments do not reflect America's traditional viewpoints, they are having an influence, pitting one citizen against another. The administration clearly views wealth creation as a distasteful pursuit, but it can accept it grudgingly as long as it has the final say in how much the wealth-creator gets to keep.

No entrepreneur I've coached goes into business for the purpose of providing the government with more tax money. What does drive entrepreneurs? This is easy for me to answer, as I have asked thousands of entrepreneurs this very question for two decades. The answer is simple and constant: freedom. This means *their freedom* to live *their way*, on *their terms*, with the only impediment to their success being their ability to achieve results. This is consistent with the Founders' vision of America providing citizens with the opportunity, but not the assurance, of improving their life without the interference of government.

The creative minority who take responsible, persistent action to fulfill their dreams often become the envy of those who stand by and just watch, report, or criticize. Left out of the popular debate are the endless stories of true American enterprise, stories of incredible work habits, stories of entrepreneurs scarred by years of sacrifice, stories of individuals overcoming obstacles and thousands of other efforts hidden from view that, brick by brick, build the American Dream.

THE THRILL OF VICTORY, THE AGONY OF DE-TAX

The president is certainly living the American Dream. So why does he rag on fellow Americans who are doing the same thing in their own way? Wouldn't everyone like to become rich and powerful like him?

In politics, envy is usually expressed through schemes that redistribute existing wealth rather than creating new wealth. And keep in mind that the "rich" who are expected to supply all this wealth are increasingly defined as anyone simply doing better than average.

This type of political warfare is toxic to the American spirit. Goethe wrote, "Divide and rule, the politician cries; unite and lead, is watchword of the wise."[14] Every time he evokes the "rich-card" or "class-card," President Obama levels a cheap shot at the American Dream, a low blow to the responsible, hard-working, and disciplined producers. It is a deeply cynical message: out of one side of his mouth, Obama speaks of hope for a prosperous future. Out of the other side, he blasts the folks who have achieved that prosperity. How can you have it both ways?

During his presidential campaign, Obama repeatedly declared that the rich were not paying their fare share. This wasn't an original ploy, but it was still a remarkable assessment given the facts: in 2007, the richest 1 percent of taxpayers paid 40 percent of all federal income taxes. The richest 5 percent paid 61 percent. The top 10 percent paid 71 percent, the top 25 percent paid 87 percent, and the top half paid a massive 97 percent of all federal income taxes. The bottom 50 percent paid hardly any at all.[15]

As opposed to the rich not paying their share, the top producers and job creators are actually being singled out and penalized. And where did this idea come from? Karl Marx, in the *Communist Manifesto*, proposed a graduated income tax as a key measure to bring about Communism, but such a tax is never advocated in the Bible. And in fact, under a flat tax, if you make more money, then you already pay higher taxes. I call this the 10-year-old test of right and wrong. It's just common sense.

If the rich are not paying their share even under a graduated income tax, then I wonder what Obama would consider to be fair? Do the top 10 percent of earners have to pay 70 percent of the total tax burden instead of just 60 percent? How about 80 percent? Or should they just pay it all? These are not mere rhetorical questions. In May 2009, the new president said, "We're beginning to restore fairness and balance to our tax code."[16] It's

WHO PAYS THE TAXES?

PERCENTILES RANKED BY AGI	ADJUSTED GROSS INCOME THRESHOLD ON PERCENTILES	PERCENTAGE OF FEDERAL PERSONAL INCOME TAX PAID
Top 1%	$388,806	39.89%
Top 5%	$153,542	60.14%
Top 10%	$108,904	70.79%
Top 25%	$64,702	86.27%
Top 50%	$31,987	97.01%
Bottom 50%	< $31,987	2.99%

Source: IRS (Tax Year 2006)

SUMMARY OF FEDERAL INDIVIDUAL INCOME TAX DATA 2007

	NUMBER OF RETURNS WITH POSITIVE AGI	AGI ($ MILLIONS)	INCOME TAXES PAID ($ MILLIONS)	GROUP'S SHARE OF TOTAL AGI	GROUP'S SHARE OF INCOME TAXES	INCOME SPLIT POINT	AVERAGE TAX RATE
All Taxpayers	141,070,971	8,798,500	1,115,504	100%	100%	–	12.68%
Top 1%	1,410,710	2,008,259	450,926	22.83%	40.42%	> $410,096	22.45%
Top 5%	7,053,549	3,294,542	676,293	37.44%	60.63%	> $160,041	20.53%
Top 10%	14,107,097	4,227,839	794,432	48.05%	71.22%	> $113,018	18.79%
Top 25%	35,267,743	6,045,354	965,875	68.71%	86.59%	> $66,532	15.98%
Top 50%	70,535,486	7,720,213	1,083,243	87.74%	97.11%	> $32,879	14.03%
Bottom 50%	70,535,485	1,078,287	32,261	12.26%	2.89%	< $32,879	2.99%

Source: Internal Revenue Service

reasonable to ask what exactly his final goal of a "fair" tax code will be.

There seems to be a bitter premise in the psyche of President Obama and other redistributionists. They believe that the successful have either unjustly earned their money at the expense of others or that they were simply lucky. Either way, fairness requires spreading this money around to the other people who were exploited or who weren't as lucky. The bottom line is that you, the earner, were either bad or lucky, so you're not entitled to the money in your possession. And truthfully, many redistributionists don't really believe the rich are just lucky. They just promote that message to increase the sense of envy.

Redistribution is not a poverty-fighting strategy, it's a calculating political strategy. It creates predictable constituencies for future election cycles. Who would vote for the candidate that might turn off or even slow down the faucet of free money? This is one of the reasons the framers opposed such practices; it inevitably corrupts the system.

The president believes in redistributing wealth in order to achieve so-called "economic justice," or as a form of "reparative economic work." These phrases should cause alarm, as they are code words for socialism. Obama also has indicated that he believes the Constitution to be fundamentally flawed, and that the U.S. Supreme Court erred by refusing to mandate redistribution.[17] And of course, his widely-broadcast remark to Joe the Plumber highlights the audacity of his conviction. When Joe voiced concern that Obama would raise his taxes, Obama replied,

> It's not that I want to punish your success. I want to make sure that everybody who is behind you, that they've got a chance for success, too.... My attitude is that if the economy's good for folks from the bottom up, it's gonna be good for everybody.... I think when you spread the wealth around, it's good for everybody.[18]

Obama and other statists believe that if you earn "too much," then it's not really your money. Whose is it? That's easy—it's the government's money. In other words, it's *their* money, and they'll spread it around to whomever they like.

According to an old saying, the problem with class warfare is that sooner or later you run out of productive people's money. Successful people already pay a wildly disproportionate share of taxes. And at some point, if you demonize them enough and confiscate enough of their wealth, you reduce everyone's incentive to become successful in the first place. Most people think of this as "killing the goose that lays the golden egg." But the Obama administration sees it as a primary goal.

ATHLETIC JUSTICE?

By vowing to punish financial success through higher taxes, the Obama administration is endorsing mediocrity. It's like taxing a gold medal winner in the Olympics—we could call it "The Phelps Tax," after swimming sensation Michael Phelps. Imagine that gold medal winners must have their medals melted down and redistributed to the second and third place finishers, whose own medals would be redistributed to those who won no medals at all. This would certainly spread the wealth around. What do you think? Are we headed in this direction? Maybe we could call this "Athletic Justice." The fact that Phelps had a clear goal, outworked his competition, and made maximum use of his God-given talent is immaterial. It simply isn't fair that one athlete should have so much success when so many lesser athletes have to return home with no medal at all.

In reality, just as the Olympic gold is best worn by Michael Phelps, money is best spent by the individual who earned it. Most Americans would admire Phelps's success, not seek to diminish it out of envy. That's because envy is foreign to the American character. As Thomas Jefferson wrote, "To take from one, because it is thought that his own industry and that of his father's has acquired too much, in order to spare others, who, or whose fathers have not exercised equal industry and skill, is to violate arbitrarily the first principle of association—the guarantee to everyone of his industry and the fruits acquired by it."[19]

Decades later Abraham Lincoln commented, "That some should be rich shows that others may become rich, and hence is just encouragement to industry and enterprise. Let not him who is houseless pull down the house of another; but let him labor diligently and build one for himself, thus by example assuring that his own shall be safe from violence when built."[20]

President Calvin Coolidge spoke along the same lines, observing, "The wise and correct course to follow in taxation and all other economic legislation is not to destroy those who have already secured success but to create conditions under which everyone will have a better chance to be successful." These words speak to the distinctively American mindset.

What citizen can possibly think that class envy is a good thing for the moral fiber of our country or the integrity of the individuals involved? What American can claim that pitting one group of people against another is patriotic?

Americans are the most generous, giving, and compassionate people on the planet. We all want to help and support those who are needy and deserving. But we don't reach new heights as a nation by poisoning the spirit and the vision of success. We cannot be for something and against it simultaneously—we cannot be for success and then vilify the successful individual.

WHOOPS, WHERE DID THE WEALTH GO?

Putting aside the moral issue, everyone needs to understand the practical consequences of redistribution schemes. Before the government can redistribute another citizen's wealth, that citizen must be highly productive and earn enough wealth to be redistributed. Once this citizen begins to lose what he has rightly earned, the incentive to produce and excel in the future diminishes. The entire scheme punishes the successful, but it also inevitably causes the bottom to fall out from under the recipients of the free money. Over time, there is simply less and less to distribute.

No American likes high taxes, especially with the atrocious record of government inefficiency in handling our tax dollars. And raising tax rates on the most productive inevitably harms the rest of the population. The job creators raise prices on their goods and services to offset the projected loss, just as businesses factor in their corporate tax liability when setting prices for their products.

Since the days of the Boston Tea Party, Americans have always been extremely sensitive to high taxes. For example, researchers Arthur Laffer and Stephen Moore found,

> from 1998 to 2007, more than 1100 people everyday including Sundays and holidays moved from the nine highest income tax states such as California, New Jersey, New York, and Ohio and relocated mostly to the nine tax-haven states with no income tax, including Florida, Nevada, New Hampshire and Texas. We also found that over these same years the no-income tax states created 89 percent more jobs and had 32 percent faster personal income growth than their high-tax counterparts.[21]

And that was no anomaly. One way or another, wealthy Americans find creative ways to avoid losing their wealth to overreaching bureaucrats. Following large income tax hikes on the wealthy in Connecticut, New Jersey, and New York, studies found a significant reduction in the number of rich people paying taxes relative to the national average. In fact, these three states ranked 46th, 49th, and 50th out of all states in wealthy tax filers after the increase was introduced.[22] Even more examples are easy to find. As reported in the *Wall Street Journal*, when Maryland tried to balance its budget by soaking the rich, the successful fled the state for tax friendlier spots like Florida, South Carolina, and Virginia, leaving the middle class to make up the difference.[23]

Economics professors Christina and David Romer found that, as a rule, higher taxes diminish economic activity modestly at first and then more rapidly within a couple of years. Thus, a tax increase of 1 percent of GDP lowers GDP by about 3 percent. According to the Romers' findings, "Tax increases appear to have a very large, sustained and highly significant negative impact on output." Conversely, their research found that "tax cuts have very large and persistent positive output effects."[24]

Dr. J. D. Foster of the Heritage Foundation reached a similar conclusion: "Clear and compelling evidence shows that higher taxes have multiple harmful effects on the economy."[25] And the great Winston Churchill also pontificated on the subject, arguing that "for a nation to try to tax itself into prosperity is like a man standing in a bucket and trying to lift himself up by the handle."

As shown throughout this chapter, a lot of presidents, statesmen, and researchers have commented on the futility of high taxes, class envy, and wealth redistribution. But perhaps the argument was summed up best by a journalist and author, P. J. O'Rourke:

> The first Nine Commandments concern theological principles and social law. But then, right at the end, is "Don't envy your buddy's cow." How did that make the top ten? What's it doing there? Why would God, with just ten things to tell Moses, choose as one of those things jealousy about the starter mansion with in-ground pool next door?
>
> Yet think how important the Tenth Commandment is to a community, to a nation, indeed to a presidential election. If you want a mule, if you want a pot roast, if you want a cleaning lady, don't be a jerk and whine about what the people across the street have—go get your own.

The Tenth Commandment sends a message to all the jerks who want redistribution of wealth, higher taxes, more government programs, more government regulation, more government, less free enterprise, and less freedom. And the message is clear and concise: Go to hell.[26]

It appears, however, that President Obama aims to break the "51 percent barrier." Previously thought impossible in America, this refers to a political strategy of relieving over half the population of paying any net taxes whatsoever. The goal is to create a voting majority that is permanently wedded to one political party. The minority that actually funds the government will then become a politically irrelevant sub-group, more like subjects than citizens. This is very close to happening right now. We are close to moving irreversibly into a new society where excellence does not pay, and success is punished, discouraged, and virtually abolished as a result.

CHAPTER FIVE

EXERCISE IN A BOTTLE

"The world doesn't owe you a thing. It was here first."

—MARK TWAIN

THE POWER-GRABBING SCHEME of penalizing the successful and re-appropriating their assets would never have gotten off the ground in America unless it were fueled by the natural human tendency to try to get something for free. As Thomas Jefferson noted, "The worst day in a man's life is when he sits down and begins thinking about how he can get something for nothing."

And it follows that the worst day in a country's history is the day when the majority of its citizens vote to approve this "something for nothing" way of life. Alexis de Tocqueville warned, "The American Republic will endure until the day Congress discovers that it can bribe the public with the public's money." For us, that day may have been November 4, 2008.

As explained in the next chapter, on that day the American people did not knowingly vote for the destructive agenda that Obama has adopted. Nevertheless, Election Day 2008 marked a fateful advance of the character plague that is sweeping across the nation. It is our next statitude—*the "something for nothing" epidemic.*

The United States government is the primary culprit, handing out free money with no strings attached. Supposedly victimized identity groups and other special interests have become the strung out users addicted to government largess. And most of us are involuntarily financing the spread of the disease with our tax dollars. Lately, the government has even infected corporate America. Companies that made poor decisions are being "bailed out" with taxpayer dollars—in other words, they're being rescued from facing the consequences of their own actions.

As Cal Thomas wrote, "The president's economic doctrine subsidizes people who make wrong decisions and does little to encourage them to make the right ones. Failure becomes an option, the flip side of success. One can make money either way."[1] Of course, this is a win-win policy for President Obama—he expands the government's role in the economy while striking a devastating blow for the War on Success.

HOPE, CHANGE, AND EXERCISE IN A BOTTLE

Let's take a look at one small example of what happens when people try to get something for nothing.

Several years ago, a hip, new nutritional supplement arrived on the scene and brought hope to millions of Americans who were struggling with their weight but didn't want to exercise. "Exercise in a Bottle" promised to help non-exercisers burn calories while they were standing or sitting, or even while they were sleeping, "so they would never have to exercise again."

From a marketing perspective, this was a great idea. It was easy to promote because it played to the lowest side of human nature— it offered something for nothing. It offered the potential customer what he wanted—a lean, sexy physique—without having to pay the unappealing price of hard work in the gym and self-discipline at the dinner table.

The companion product, "Fat Trapper Plus," was equally enticing. It claimed to block the absorption of fat permanently so users could eat "fried chicken, pizza, cheeseburgers . . . and stop worrying about the weight." The infomercial showed images of attractive men and women in their bathing suits chowing down on a buffet of fried chicken, burgers, breads, and desserts.

The brilliant marketing, however, masked a serious drawback: the product didn't work. In 2005, the Federal Trade Commission charged the manufacturer with making unsubstantiated weight-loss claims and misrepresenting scientific studies.[2] In the end, people who bought "Exercise in a Bottle" didn't get something for nothing—they just got ripped off.

And that should come as no surprise. The "something for nothing" ethos doesn't work in our personal lives, and it doesn't work in business. It doesn't work as national policy either, because no one can get anything for free unless someone else produces it. If that productive class steadily diminishes—which is the goal of the War on Success—then eventually we run out of goodies to give to everyone. This is a simple lesson, but we never learn it. Amazingly, Cornell's Weill Medical Center is currently studying a new medication that simulates exercise in the body[3]—it's just another "Exercise in the Bottle."

Everyone has a natural desire to get something for nothing, but this is an urge we should resist. Instead, our government is deliberately cultivating this mindset. The late American pastor Adrian Rogers explained the dire risks this poses:

> What one person receives without working for, another person must work for without receiving. The government cannot give to anybody anything that the government does not first take from somebody else. When half of the people get the idea that they do not have to work because the other half is going to take care of them, and when the other half gets the idea that it does

no good to work because somebody else is going to get what they work for, that my dear friend, is about the end of any nation. You cannot multiply wealth by dividing it.[4]

The "something for nothing" statitude robs Americans of our initiative and entrepreneurial energy. It is a ludicrous inversion of the traditional American work ethic—one that could have the most calamitous repercussions on the whole nation.

MAKE IT OR TAKE IT

There is only one way for us to create wealth and that is to be productive, meaning that we create something of value in the economy. However, there are two ways to get just about anything we want in life. The first method is to earn it. This is what nearly all of us were taught—we can think of this as the American way. The second approach—the one preferred by the Obama administration—is to take it from someone who has earned it and claim it as your own. Joe Biden articulated so clearly the administration's intentions when he told *Good Morning America*, "We want to *take money* and put it back in the pocket of middle-class people." He added, "It's time to be patriotic...time to jump in, time to be part of the deal, time to help get America out of the rut"[5] (emphasis added).

The vice president, however, has not been so "patriotic" with his own money, donating just $995 to charity in 2007 and $1,885 in 2008—less than 1 percent of his income. And he gave even less in previous years.[6] So from whom are we supposed to be "taking money"? Biden didn't specify, but apparently it's not from him.

Having a fairly old-fashioned upbringing, I grew up knowing that the second approach is called stealing—whether the government sanctions it or not. For example, imagine if Congress passed a law allowing pick pocketing as long as the victim was wealthy (or appeared to be wealthy) and the assailant was needy, deserving, or just less fortunate than the victim. From a moral perspective, would this no longer be theft simply because the government allows it?

Imagine if one of my neighbors had three cars, and I had a friend who only had one but really needed a second vehicle for taking the kids to school or some other worthwhile cause. My friend clearly needs another car, and my neighbor clearly has plenty of cars for one family, right? Would it then be acceptable if I took my neighbor's third car and gave it to my friend? As John Locke noted, "The people cannot delegate to government the power to do anything which would be unlawful for them to do themselves."

Free money is cruelty dressed up as sympathy—it robs one group of people and fosters a debilitating dependence in another. Yet, the government is handing out an ever-growing hoard of other people's money. Obama's $787 billion "stimulus" bill was a historic bonanza of free money for deficit-ridden state and local governments, bloated universities, and well-connected companies working on "green" technologies for which there is no market demand. And if the goal of the stimulus was to reduce unemployment, as Obama claimed, it's been a total failure: since Obama signed the stimulus bill in February 2009, unemployment has shot up from 8.1 percent to 10.2 percent.

But the stimulus *has* been successful in deepening the notion that if you've got the right contacts in Washington, then you can indeed get something for nothing. To add injury to insult, all this spending is being done with a gross indifference to those whose money and earnings make this possible.

Remember, the War on Success seeks to wipe out our sense of self-reliance. Statists don't like self-reliance—it kills their business plan. How often have you heard Barack Obama tell Americans that their success is up to them? Probably never. I've exhaustively read and reread his speeches as both candidate and president, and that kind of self-reliant message simply isn't there. That's because it conflicts with his collectivist philosophy that we rise and fall as groups, that individually we are inept and need papa government to hold our hand like a toddler being led to the toilet. To a statist, success always involves government programs paid for by fellow citizens.

The president repeatedly speaks of "the idea that everybody has a stake in the country, that we're all in it together and everybody's got a shot at opportunity."[7] But how does everybody have a stake in the country if barely half are paying income tax and millions more receive free money from others via the federal government?

WHERE'S MINE?

All of us cringe when we see a young child mired in poverty. We hate to see anyone, whether young or old, suffering from want. It's difficult at times to make sense out of why some have such abundance and others struggle.

In America, some live in housing projects while others luxuriate in mansions—it seems so unfair. We see crowds on public buses and others with a spare car in their private garage. There is a natural instinct to want to end the disparity once and for all. This desire to help is normal and good. But the real issue is *how* to help—specifically, how to help one citizen without impinging on the freedom of another. The government should not provide fish for its people at the risk of never teaching them how to fish.

But our government has been providing "fish" in the form of handouts, transfer payments, and other entitlements since the 1960s. And the results conclusively show that these methods don't work. The massive expansion of the welfare state, known as the "War on Poverty," resulted in catastrophic family breakdown, skyrocketing rates of illegitimacy, and soaring crime rates among the exact communities it was meant to help. The entire program was based on the "something for nothing" precept, and that's why it failed. The universe just isn't in sync with "something for nothing."

These unaffordable and addictive programs have turned their participants into a permanent underclass condemned to a lifetime of frustration and disenchantment. Welfare programs can never compensate for a loss of principles, and trendy values can never replace timeless virtue. Free money taken from the responsible and successful is wrong in principle, but the biggest victims are the recipients who come to believe that's how the world works.

Unsurprisingly, President Obama's stimulus contained more than $80 billion in assorted welfare spending. But who's he kidding? Who believes more free money is going to create "real change"? It's not change at all—it's just repeating more of the same thing that hasn't worked before.

Here are some of the lies the poor are told:

- You need the government's help.
- No one expects you to make it on your own.
- Because others are rich, you are poor.
- You are a victim.

These lies become self-fulfilling beliefs. We can do better than this. Helping people get back on their feet and become productive is an admirable aim. But simply handing out government checks provides no long term solution, just the seemingly never-ending flow of liberty out of one person's wallet into another's. It robs the recipients of their work ethic and their dignity, often turning them into wards of the state who become experts at one thing: gaming the system. And it's a real injustice that liberals who are responsible for all this lay claim to the mantle of "compassion." After all, what reveals greater compassion—keeping people on welfare or leading them away from it?

Eradicating the "something for nothing" statitude will not be easy. Every attempt to do so elicits indignant accusations of callowness and cruelty from the interest groups that drink from the government trough, and from the politicians who protect their largess. As the late columnist Linda Bowles observed, "The task

THE DECLARATION OF DEPENDENCE

I _____, hereby willingly surrender my future choices to the infallible wisdom of the federal government of the United States of America. It is now obvious to me that the Constitution is old-fashioned, outdated, and unsuitable for our sophisticated, modern state.

From this point forward, I am a completely dependent and proud member of my assigned demographic subgroup. I understand that I rise and fall together with this very ordinary assortment of citizens.

With new enlightenment, I now release and relieve myself from the stress and uncertainty caused by pursuing my unique strengths and trying to make important life decisions on my own. I have come to understand that my risk-taking and independent ways are nothing more than an expression of selfishness. Taking initiative and being resourceful only hurts the feelings of others unwilling to take charge of their own lives.

I now recognize that I am a victim, not only of my environment, but of our capitalist society. I now see that I have been manipulated, exploited and devalued by greedy, free-market businesspeople who seek unfairness by investing their time wisely and practicing an unreasonable work ethic year after year.

Free of the anxiety that accompanies ambition, I look forward to an appropriately average future full of routine, sameness, and predictability, and I promise, if convenient, to dedicate at least twenty-nine hours each week, forty-two weeks of the year to developing my equal-ness in all areas of my life. This conditional commitment will guarantee happy feelings for all members of my subgroup, as long as we all shall live.

of weaning various people and groups from the national nipple will not be easy. The sound of whines, bawls, screams, and invective will fill the air as the agony of withdrawal pangs finds voice."[8]

The dilemma over government welfare is nothing new—it goes back to the country's founding. And Ben Franklin had some simple, wise advice:

> I am for doing good to the poor, but I differ in opinion of the means. I think the best way of doing good to the poor, is not making them easy in poverty, but leading or driving them out of it. In my youth I travelled much, and I observed in different countries, that the more public provisions were made for the poor, the less they provided for themselves, and of course became poorer. And, on the contrary, the less was done for them, the more they did for themselves, and became richer.

So how do we responsibly help those in need? First, we have to distinguish between the deserving poor and the undeserving poor. Everyone wants to help those who are incapable of helping themselves, as well as those who are making an honest effort to become self-reliant, productive members of society. However, while politically incorrect, we must face the truth that welfare enables and even encourages irresponsible behavior and contributes to a permanent underclass. This is not a secret to anyone paying attention. Trillions of dollars later, it's clear that money can't fix human nature.

Nonetheless, too many statists seek to treat the symptoms of neediness rather than address the root causes. The liberal welfare philosophy is rooted in the errant assumption that one's lot in life is static and we must therefore, as a society, help those "permanently stuck" in poverty to cope and be as comfortable as possible. We must steer clear of this defeatist thinking and believe in the power of the individual to overcome his circumstances with a temporary hand up, not a permanent handout. We must make it clear that government assistance is a short-term measure, and benefits should progressively decrease over time. In the final chapter, we'll discuss some concrete policies for helping the poor to transcend their circumstances instead of merely coping with them.

POLITICAL CORRECTNESS: THE JOY OF NEWSPEAK

It is deeply entrenched in our government, throughout the media, within our educational system, in many scientific circles, and in the corporate workplace. It erodes our culture from within, as the citizens of this nation sheepishly censor themselves and surrender their freedom of thought, speech, and expression. It is called *political correctness*, and it is our final statitude.

Here's what a politically correct conversation sounds like: "I'm offended that you're offended, and no doubt you'll be offended that I'm offended because you're offended. But that's the truth because that's what I'm feeling right now."

Good grief! Who among us has not laughed at politically correct absurdity? Come on now. You had to laugh (or maybe cry) when officials in Washington state authorized a display honoring "Festivus"—a mock, alternative holiday to Christmas originating in a *Seinfeld* episode—alongside the Nativity and other religious displays at the state Capitol. (The governor eventually vetoed the Festivus display, though an atheist display remained. By the way, what exactly do atheists display, anyway?)

Political correctness is all about showing a comical level of sensitivity toward certain identity groups. One of its main features is renaming groups of people and certain concepts to avoid giving offense. Let's warm up this discussion with some familiar examples. In order to banish "sexism" from the English language, "flight attendant" replaced "stewardess," and "server" is now preferred over "waiter" or "waitress." "Fireman," of course, had to go, so that became "fireperson" and then "firefighter." "Freshman" was a little trickier—in lieu of "fresh-persons," it was replaced with the awkward concoction, "incoming first year student."

Many moons ago, "Indian" was replaced with "Native American," though some Indians apparently object to the term because it "linguistically eradicates" the history of their oppression by whites.[9] (Please note if you meet someone actually from the country of India, you may, both accurately and politely, refer to them as Indian.) And once they cross the border, Mexicans transform into "Latinos" or "Chicanos," though if they're illegal immigrants, there's a new designation recently introduced by Vice President Joe Biden—"undocumented visitors."

In the same spirit, "handicapped" people became "disabled" before we were retrained to call them "differently-abled," and then "physically challenged." And blind people are now "sightless" or "vision impaired," although a visually impaired friend of mine calls me "blind-less." That feels to me like a slight of some sort, but I've decided to be okay with it for now. Oh, and "hardworking Americans" is the PC designation for blue collar workers—as though doctors, lawyers, teachers, corporate executives, and small business owners don't really work so hard.

Religion is a particularly delicate topic. "BC" or "Before Christ" is out, and "BCE" or "Before the Common Era" is in. Also, if you must refer to your spirituality or religious beliefs, the courteous term is now "religious tradition"—unless you happen to be Christian, in which case your faith is usually referred to as "the oppressor." Mind you, these terms change frequently—by the time this book hits the shelves, there'll probably be new names for all of the above, except that last one.

Despite this silliness, political correctness is not as benign as you may think—in fact, some aspects of political correctness are downright threatening to our entire society. Let me explain with a little bit of history.

THE ROOTS OF POLITICAL CORRECTNESS

Political correctness does not trace back to the Founders of our nation or their holy inspiration, but to the early 1920s in both Bolshevik Russia and pre-Nazi Germany. Its concepts were developed by the notorious "Frankfurt School," a group of Marxist intellectuals working at a think tank at Germany's University of Frankfurt. Seeking to learn why socialism wasn't spreading from Russia as fast as predicted and desired, the academics concluded that independent thinking and other elements of Western culture were slowing the transformation. Western thought seemed to be filled with the "belief in the individual" and was resistant to the collective wisdom of state planners.

Their solution was to undermine that stubborn Western tradition via the practice of "critical theory." This is the strategy of vilifying traditional thinking—or any belief system, set of facts, or historical truths—that contradicts socialism. In other words, political correctness is an ideology designed to weaken traditional Western culture and Judeo-Christian customs as a preamble to full-blown Communism.

After Hitler came to power in 1935, the Frankfurt School moved to New York City, where it began translating economic Marxism into its cultural counterpart using Sigmund Freud's psychological conditioning mechanisms.[10] Thus, political correctness is accurately portrayed as "cultural Marxism," because it softens or readies the culture for egalitarian ideals. It is employed to devalue the tenets of Western civilization: capitalism, the traditional family, Western religious beliefs, and in our case, American exceptionalism. Arguments in favor of these traditions are denounced as "offensive," declared to be "beyond the pale" of debate, and written out of the English language. This corrosive ideology spread throughout American universities, especially from the early 1980s, and from there seeped into the media, government, and most other facets of American life.

As a result of political correctness, certain topics, expressions, and even gestures have been declared off-limits. The guidelines and rules of political correctness read like a new age religious pamphlet. Who comes up with these directives for what's allowable and what's off limits? We don't really know. Fortunately, the PC gods keep the media and our schools up to date on all the changes.

WOULDN'T IT BE GREAT IF...

1. We could have a lot of money but not have to work for it

2. We could be healthy and fit without having to exercise or discipline our appetite

3. We could have a wonderful marriage without even trying

4. Our kids could make straight A's without having to study

5. We could fall off a cliff and go up, not down

6. We never had to grow up

7. We could live in a land of make believe

I see no value in needlessly offending someone, and you probably don't either. But I find it a tad bit spineless for people to censor themselves out of fear of being insensitive. It's inspiring to see someone stand up, go out on a limb, and take a stand on meaningful things. It's the American way. There are issues that need to be discussed openly and freely without the filter of political correctness. When certain words, ideas, and points of view are banned from discussion, the result is a stifling intellectual conformity. It's therefore a supreme irony that political correctness is often spread under the slogan of "diversity" and "tolerance."

Apparently, we need every kind of "diversity" except diversity of thought, and we should "tolerate" every belief except belief in traditional values.

This struggle to be politically correct has made regular people hyper-sensitive to their own words and to the words of others. We're becoming a society that walks on eggshells, scared to kid around, get personal, and be real with each other out of fear of accidentally saying something distasteful.

In the PC universe, those who have the audacity to break ranks and stand up for their convictions are labeled with charming words like "narrow-minded," "intolerant," "extremist," "bigot," "racist," "homophobe," and my favorite, "xenophobe." To judge in any way another's behavior or choices equates to "hating them." To avoid being called one of those nasty names, we need to remember that "nothing is wrong, just different."

This moral equivalence is the hallmark of political correctness—and it's a key weapon in the War on Success.

I DREAM OF AN UNHYPHENATED AMERICA!

Political correctness is closely associated with multiculturalism, a doctrine that celebrates and promotes foreign cultures within the United States. Rejecting America's melting-pot tradition, this unprincipled philosophy encourages immigrants to retain their native culture in the name of "diversity." Multiculturalists believe it's immoral to criticize any culture—except, of course, Western culture, and especially American culture, which is condemned as being exploitive and racist. But aside from our own culture, all cultures are equally good, according to the multiculturalist. Ultimately, the ideology boils down to a destructive kind of nihilism, since when we believe in everything, we might as well believe in nothing.

The "melting pot" intention of our Founders, expressed on our currency with the motto *e pluribus Unum*—"Out of many, one"—welcomes foreigners into our culture expecting them to assimilate our ways and traditions. From many backgrounds we become one strong nation. Once you hit our shores, only three colors should matter: red, white, and blue! How can our country ever be united if we are split up into special groups? Why can't we have an unhyphenated America?

Today, patriotic Americans are not "anti-immigrant" but "pro-America." We welcome immigrants who are hard-working, law-abiding, and willing to learn English. What's to be gained by having lesser standards than these? Even Teddy Roosevelt, an early Progressive, felt strongly about this, insisting:

> There can be no divided allegiance here. Any man who says he is an American, but something else also, isn't an American at all. We have room for but one flag, the American flag. We have room for but one language here, and that is the English language... and we have room for but one sole loyalty and that is a loyalty to the American people.[11]

Is this really a radical notion? Not according to the American people, who overwhelmingly support patriotic assimilation over multiculturalism:

- Eighty percent of U.S. citizens believe those who move to America should adopt American culture rather than flaunt their home culture.[12]
- Eighty-four percent of Americans think English should be the official language of the United States.[13] Sixty-five percent of Hispanics agree.[14]

- Seventy-nine percent of Americans believe immigrants should be required to learn English before becoming citizens. Only 14 percent disagree.[15]
- By more than a 2–1 margin, immigrants themselves say the United States should expect new immigrants to learn English.[16]
- Ninety-one percent of foreign-born Hispanic immigrants agree that learning English is essential to succeed in the United States.[17]

President Obama and Vice President Biden, however, apparently have other views. They don't even support making English the official language of the United States. For them, it seems, the melting pot is just another antiquated American idea that needs to be "re-made."

WE'RE JUST TEACHING RESPECT

Under the guise of "respect" and "politeness," children are taught in school which words and phrases are acceptable to describe the world, and by extension, they're taught how to think about the world. Political correctness has infected this process, and its teachings are a far cry from ingraining "please," "thank you," "yes sir," and "no ma'am."

PC has extended into student textbooks and school curricula, especially those affiliated with the National Education Association. American history is now largely told from the perspective of minorities suffering at the hands of white oppressors. Naturally, America's Judeo-Christian heritage is virtually erased from most textbooks, unless it's used to illustrate some kind of injustice. Overall, America is described by its flaws, not its strengths, by its mistakes, not its magnificence.

This presents a clear and present danger. Children who are indoctrinated to oppose traditional American values will grow up ill-prepared to defend the principles that have made America great. Instead, they will be led down a secular, humanistic path of speculation about what should make our country great in the eyes of "our global partners," which really means, "other countries that don't share our values or principles." As Mark Steyn warned, "In the long run, the relativist mush peddled in our grade schools is a national security threat. But even in the short term, it's a form of child abuse that cuts off America's next generation from the glories of their inheritance."[18]

Directly changing how we think is quite difficult to do. We've all had experience trying to improve our thinking to better deal with an important relationship, or to better cope with adversity of some kind, or even just to become more positive. However, years of habitual thinking patterns create mental inertia that is almost impossible to dislodge, especially if we don't know how.

What we tell ourselves repeatedly, we start believing. This is what political correctness is all about, despite the fact that most people who play along with it or even promote it have no clue what they're really doing. This has an insidious influence on children as well as adults: by dictating the words we're allowed to use and how we describe what we observe every day, political correctness uses our mouths to influence our minds. This is a well-known psychological principle, but most people are unaware that going along with PC speech can reshape their entire worldview—and the fundamental values of this nation.

RUSH TO JUDGMENT

Even that all-American institution, the NFL, has ingested the Kool-Aid® of political correctness. Recently, conservative talk show host Rush Limbaugh was blocked from becoming a minority owner of the St. Louis Rams. He was ostracized because of some controversial comments he allegedly made, most of which, it turned out, he'd never actually said. The most controversial comment he *did* make was his 2003 remark that Philadelphia Eagles quarterback Donovan McNabb received so much good press because the media wanted to see a black quarterback succeed. Explaining the rejection of Limbaugh's ownership bid, NFL commissioner Roger Goodell said, "The comments Rush made specifically about Donovan, I disagree with very strongly. It's a polarizing comment that we don't think reflect accurately on the NFL or our players. I obviously do not believe those comments are positive, and they are divisive."

To put this in perspective, the NFL doesn't seem to regard Fergie or Serena Williams as divisive—they both share minority stakes in the Miami Dolphins. Let's take a brief look at the resume they bring to the league:

- Black Eyed Peas singer Stacy Ferguson, aka "Fergie," sings, "Overseas, yeah, we try to stop terrorism/But we still got terrorists livin'/In the USA, the big CIA/The Bloods and the Crips and the KKK."[19]
- Serena Williams was disqualified from a tennis match after unleashing an expletive-filled tirade on live TV and threatening a side judge.

And no professional sports league would be complete without the high standards of Snoop Dogg, who appeared in television ads for ESPN's *Sunday NFL Countdown* in 2009. A cursory check of Snoop's rap sheet reveals the following:

- 1993: arrested and charged with murder. He was later acquitted on grounds of self-defense.

- 1997: pled guilty to one count of being an ex-felon in possession of a handgun
- 1998 and 2001: fined and arrested for misdemeanor marijuana possession
- April 2006: vandalized a duty-free shop at Heathrow Airport. He was later denied entry to the UK for the foreseeable future.
- October 2006: arrested on firearm and drug possession charges
- November 2006: arrested for possession of marijuana and a firearm
- 2007: temporarily banned from Australia due to prior criminal convictions
- 2009: sued for assaulting a fan on stage at a May 2005 concert

Now I ask you: is Limbaugh's belief that the media hypes McNabb really more "divisive" than verbally abusing and threatening a line judge, accusing the CIA of terrorism, or committing any of the crimes Snoop Dogg has? It seems the NFL's "high-standards" are really double standards. So much for "tolerance."

THE GREATER DANGER

Although it's promoted casually as a means to civil discourse, political correctness has evolved into blatant speech control. This is especially true on many college campuses where "speech codes" mandate which words and expressions are allowed and which are banned. Shouldn't these institutions have the freest exchange of ideas and perspectives? This doesn't exactly create a friendly environment for critical thought, does it? And funny enough, prior to the boom of political correctness in the early 1980s and 1990s, what "intolerance" and "incivility" there was on college campuses came mostly from the radical Left—that is, from the same people who are now tenured professors and college administrators, busy lassoing speech codes onto everyone else.

For now, formal speech codes are largely confined to college campuses. But Europe, where political correctness is more advanced, indicates our trajectory. Across the Atlantic, the trend is simply to outlaw "offensive" speech. This, for example, affected the late Italian journalist Oriana Fallaci. A former World War II partisan and world-renowned journalist, Fallaci wrote a book criticizing Islamic practices and was indicted by an Italian court in 2002 for "defaming Islam." Luckily, before she was indicted she moved to America, where we don't have those kinds of defamation laws—yet.[20] Europe's experience is particularly noteworthy because our current administration has an affinity for emulating the continent's customs and repeating its mistakes.

The threat to free speech is bad enough, but political correctness even threatens our national security. We are now engaged in a worldwide war against Islamic terrorists, yet political correctness prevents us from understanding our enemies or even naming them. Because it's "insensitive" and "intolerant" to point out that our enemies are inspired by Islam and justify their attacks by citing Islamic scripture, our government continually tries to white-wash Islam out of the picture. The Obama administration even found "the global war on terror" to be insensitive, so it's been given the ridiculous euphemism of "overseas contingency operation."

This politically-correct deference to Islam has already produced the most horrific results. In November 2009, a U.S. Army psychiatrist, Major Nidal M. Hasan, went on a bloody rampage at Fort Hood, massacring fourteen people including an unborn baby. Hasan had a disturbing record as a radical Muslim—he proselytized Islam to his patients, turned his medical lectures into discourses about jihad, and had "SoA," or "Soldier of Allah," printed on his business cards. Authorities even investigated him for communicating with a radical jihadist preacher in Yemen. Yet, despite all the warning signs, everyone was too afraid to remove him—who wants to be vilified as a racist or an "Islamophobe"? As an official at the Walter Reed Army Medical Center said of Hasan's medical residency there, "Some of the [policy committee] members sat around saying, 'And how would it look if we kick out one of the few Muslim residents in our program?'"[21]

The media's reaction to the massacre was drenched in political correctness. From the beginning, reporters struggled not to mention Islam, even though Hasan reportedly screamed "Allahu Akbar"—the jihadist battle cry—during the attack. They claimed he was just "psychotic" or that he'd been picked on, and they even invented a new psychiatric illness—"secondary post-traumatic stress disorder"—to account for his actions. The notion that Islam had anything to do with it was simply not acceptable.

Hasan's dreadful massacre makes one thing crystal clear: political correctness is an ideology that many powerful people are willing to sacrifice for—right down to the last American soldier.

THE BLIND LEADING THE BLIND

It's not that all PC practitioners are part of some vast conspiracy; most are just doing what they're told, playing along with what's in vogue, swept up in the whirlwind of what everyone else is doing. Like wearing certain clothes simply because they're fashionable, most people who play along with PC are innocently following the leader.

America is in the middle of being "re-made." It can be difficult to see the whole picture when we are inside the frame, busy with our own lives. But we are heading rapidly toward a highly centralized statist government with unprecedented reach and authoritative power in how we run our life. Uncertainty about our nation's future is at an all-time high. With the new administration, political correctness is picking up speed and taking its toll on traditional values, paving the way for un-American attitudes to rush in.

Propelled by political correctness, the seeds of doubt and confusion about our nation's history and goodness are being planted inside and outside our borders. How did we get to the point where "being inoffensive" supersedes speaking the truth? The answer is that we've hardly done anything to stop it.

Political correctness is a mighty foe, but once in a while its excesses become so outrageous that the public rebels. After the September 11 attacks, the iconic photograph of New York firefighters raising the American flag over the ruins of the World Trade Center was going to be turned into a memorial sculpture. But the forces of political correctness intervened and insisted on replacing some of the white firefighters with minorities. As it turned out, this crass exploitation of September 11 to advance political correctness was just too much, and the plans were scrapped amid an outcry from both the firemen and the general public.[22]

Political correctness can be stopped and even reversed. But it's going to take courage—the courage to speak the truth. One of the wacky dynamics of PC is that people will often feel too intimidated to speak out at a public meeting, and then privately share their concerns with others later. One of the most powerful things we can do to defend the great traditions of this country is to exercise our courage and speak out at cookouts, parties, school board meetings, and townhalls, so that like-minded people will see they have allies in their battle for freedom.

Accusations of racism and intolerance are incredibly effective, intimidating many people into cowed silence about the crucial issues of our day. It takes a lot of guts to say what you believe, knowing you will be met with howls of outrage and personal invective. We should take heart from an old saying of Winston Churchill: "You have enemies? Good. That means you've stood up for something, sometime in your life."

CHAPTER SIX

A KINDER, GENTLER MARXISM

"A new revolution is possible only in consequence of a new crisis."

—KARL MARX

THE TIME HAS COME TO DISCUSS the particular kind of statism that enamors the Obama administration: socialism.

Before we begin, we should define the key term used here. Socialism is one of several statist philosophies; the other main one is fascism, also called corporatism. What the various statist philosophies have in common is the overwhelming importance they attribute to a powerful central government. Back in the 1930s, historian Walter Lippman commented on this fetish for state power that binds different statist tendencies: "Throughout the world, in the name of progress, men who call themselves communists, socialists, fascists, nationalists, progressives and even liberals, are unanimous in holding that government with its instruments of coercion, must by commanding the people how they shall live, direct the course of civilization and fix the shape of things to come."[1]

Socialism seeks to make all citizens economically equal through forcibly redistributing wealth, minimizing private property rights, and maximizing state control of the economy. To the greatest extent possible, a state's economy is planned or regulated by a central authority. Socialist states also typically reject Judeo-Christian values, instead attributing a semi-mystical power to the state apparatus.

As explained by Karl Marx, the final stage of socialism is Communism. This is achieved after private property is completely abolished and the state gains control of all production. At that point, according to Marx, society will function so smoothly that there will be no more need for government. In the words of Friedrich Engels, Marx's collaborator, the state "withers away," as people live together in complete harmony and equality. Although many Communist regimes have attempted to realize Marx's vision, not a single one has achieved this utopian condition, and not a single Communist government has "withered away." The common result—from the USSR to Cambodia to North Korea—has been grinding poverty, a complete loss of freedom, and mass murder.

With these terms and this historical record in mind, let's look at the Obama administration's attempts to implant socialism in America.

STRIKING WHILE THE IRON IS HOT

In order to drag America into socialism, Obama and his supporters portray America as a place of atrocious poverty and injustice that can only be rectified by massive government intervention. This tactic was recommended by Saul Alinsky, the consummate theoretician of American radicalism, who taught, "Any revolutionary change must be preceded by a passive, affirmative, non-challenging attitude toward change among the mass of our people. They must feel so frustrated, so defeated, so lost, so futureless in the prevailing system that they are willing to let go of the past and change the future. This acceptance is the reformation essential to any revolution."[2]

A rapid transition from capitalism to socialism requires a convergence of several factors:

- Crisis
- Fear
- Presence of a charismatic socialist spokesperson
- Denigration of timeless principles
- Indifference toward history

When we are really scared, it's not unlike being intoxicated. Suddenly, we become open to scenarios and proposals we would never entertain if sober. And that's what happened during the 2008 financial crisis, when all the key elements listed above suddenly converged, resulting in the election of Barack Obama. Frightened, frozen, and frustrated, many chose to believe in Obama's vague promises of "change" without understanding what he meant by that.

What Obama really had in mind was socialism. Consider what we've seen just in his first year in office—massive government intrusions into the finance and auto industries, the expansion of welfare and social programs, the government's attempt to take over healthcare, the demonization and over-regulation of business. Is it simply a coincidence that each of these policies moves us toward socialism? How many more "coincidences" do we need?

Or, to ask a slightly different question, which Obama policies *oppose* the socialist agenda? If you can think of one, it'll be one more than I can.

THE OPPOSITE OF INDIVIDUALISM IS . . .

First and foremost, socialism seeks to crush individualism. John Stuart Mill foresaw where this kind of action leads: "Whatever crushes individuality is despotism, whether it professes to be enforcing the will of God or the injunctions of men."[3]

American individualism and American exceptionalism are one and the same, and they're both targets of the Obama administration. We must face the fact that our current government does not like the idea of America putting its head above the international crowd any more than it likes ambitious Americans achieving personal success here at home. Thus, it attempts to trample both American individualism and American exceptionalism by making us more like "everyone else"—that is, more socialist. We cannot kid ourselves any longer; the more socialist America becomes, the less distinct it becomes.

Obama and his supporters denigrate America's traditions, promising "change" from the "failed dogmas of the past." They apologize for the fact that we don't march in lockstep with the rest of the world. Like an immature parent hungry for her teenager to become part of the "popular crowd," they push and promote uniformity. To our current power brokers, the words "same," "even," and "average" actually represent progress.

Our president's thinking has been shaped by radical socialists and revolutionaries like Saul Alinsky, Jeremiah Wright, William Ayers, Jim Wallis, and Rashid Khalidi, to name but a few. He is steeped in the kind of identity politics that promote victimization and collectivism. In his own memoir, *Dreams from My Father*, the 34-year-old Obama wrote, "To avoid being mistaken for a sellout, I chose my friends carefully. The more politically active black students. The foreign students. The Chicanos. The Marxist professors and structural feminists."[4]

Obama's socialist mindset is common, ordinary, and pervasive worldwide. It produces mediocre societies that are dull and grey, without vitality—a natural product of citizens who are too dependent on the state. In contrast, America's exceptionalism and "can-do" attitude are rooted in personal responsibility, individualism, and the competitive spirit. These elements, which activate the divine spark within each of us, have been the catalyst for amazing technological breakthroughs and unimaginable social and economic progress over the last 234 years.

It's time to pick a side. Do we want to be part of a group-based, socialist America, or do we want to be part of an individual-based, self-reliant America? De we want to be secure in our group affiliation, or free to soar as individuals? More important, what do we want for our grandchildren and great grandchildren? Time is of the essence—we must answer this question and then quickly take action.

THE MINORITY VOTE

Polling indicates that Americans oppose the current push for socialism.[5] According to an August 2009 Gallup poll, conservatives outnumber liberals by statistically significant margins in forty-seven of the fifty states, with the two groups statistically tied in Hawaii, Vermont, and Massachusetts. Despite the Democratic Party's political strength—seen in its majority representation in Congress and in state houses across the country—more Americans consider themselves conservative than liberal. And since even many liberals oppose socialism, it's clear that supporters of socialism comprise a small minority of Americans. Unfortunately, that minority includes our current president.

Although while campaigning Obama occasionally revealed his true intentions—most notably, with his unscripted comment to Joe the Plumber about the need to "spread the wealth around"— he did not campaign as the socialist he really is. Knowing that the American people would never elect a socialist, Obama campaigned as a "post-partisan" centrist. He distanced himself from his radical colleagues like William Ayers and Jeremiah Wright, and he promised to usher in a new era of cooperation and civility in politics. That's who the American people voted for, but in the end, that's not the president we got.

Polls show it didn't take long for Americans to realize they'd been hoodwinked. Between January and June 2009, roughly covering the first half-year of Obama's presidency, 40 percent of respondents to Gallup surveys said they are either "conservative" (31 percent) or "very conservative" (9 percent)—a four-year high. That contrasts to just 21 percent who said they're liberal (16 percent) or "very liberal" (5 percent).[6]

Despite Obama's election, we are still a center-right country. His real agenda—redistributing wealth, social leveling, class warfare, historic levels of government spending and deficits, and of course, the War on Success—was not on the ballot. If it had been, then the next State of the Union address would be delivered by President McCain.

AMERICA'S SECOND FOUNDING

The Obama administration is not the first group of Americans to work for socialism. The trend began between the late 1800s and the early 1900s, when leading intellectuals sought to address issues and challenges related to the Industrial Revolution and modern capitalism. Adopting the delightfully vague name "Progressives," this movement shoved America sharply away from its original principles into what is now called the Progressive Era.

Progressives believed that the Founders' constitutional system could not deal with the new challenges facing modern society. For better governing concepts, they looked to leftwing European trends. These included socialism first and foremost, as well as environmentalism and other movements for "social justice."

Progressivism represented a radical break from American traditions. As University of Dallas professor Thomas West writes, "Progressivism was a total rejection in theory and a partial rejection in practice, of the principles and policies on which America had been founded and on the basis of which the Civil War had

been fought and won only a few years earlier."[7] Here are some of
the key Progressive ideas:

Government-Conferred Rights Trump Natural Rights

For the Founders, natural rights were derived from natural law.
They believed our rights, held equally by all, come from our Creator and are therefore inalienable. The function of government is
to secure these rights in a constitutional framework.

Progressives cavalierly dismissed this fundamental principle;
one of their key intellectuals, John Dewey, argued, "Natural rights
and natural liberties exist only in the kingdom of mythological
zoology."[8] For the Progressive, government is the source of rights.
Progressive activist Frank Goodnow, a Columbia professor and
later president of John Hopkins University, explained,

> The rights which [an individual] possesses are, it is believed,
> conferred upon him, not by his Creator, but rather by the soci-
> ety to which he belongs. What they are is to be determined by
> the legislative authority in view of the needs of that society.
> Social expediency, rather than natural right, is thus to determine
> the sphere of individual freedom of action.[9]

Goodnow rejected theories of natural right as "worse than useless," claiming they "retard development." And Progressives had
a very practical reason for holding this view. As Dr. Ron Pestritto
of Hillsdale College explains simply, "Their focus on individual
liberty prevents the expansion of government."[10]

Unlimited Government Trumps Limited Government

The Founders insisted that government exists to protect the rights
individuals inherited from God. This naturally led to their belief

in limited government, equal rights under the law, and a strong national defense.

Laughing off these supposedly antiquated concepts, Progressives redefined "freedom" as "freedom from the limits imposed by nature and necessity." The Founders' concept of "freedom from overbearing government" was thus transformed into a right to the amenities of life. These, of course, were to be provided by government.

This crucial blurring of "freedom" and "entitlement" still characterizes the liberal and progressive mindset today. Heritage Foundation scholar Dr. Matthew Spalding explains how this shift produced today's mania for identity politics:

> [Growing dependence on government] inevitably leads to a shift from an emphasis on individual rights, inherent in the nature of each person, to a concept of rights based on the various material needs and practical demands of groups. We often speak nowadays of specific rights that are said to belong to categories of individuals defined by group characteristics. This is a misconception to say the least. From the Founders' point of view, rights are inherently possessed by each and every individual and are turned into civil rights that apply equally to all persons through the constitutional process. There are no such things as "women's rights", or "black rights", or "gay rights", just as there are no "men's rights", and "heterosexual rights."[11]

Faith in State Trumps Faith in God or the Individual

The Founders believed the God of the Bible was the author of moral law. Progressives, in contrast, replaced God with the state. Some progressives even redefined God as "human freedom achieved through the right political organization."[12] John Burgess, a political scientist who influenced many American Progressives, said the goal of the state is the "perfection of humanity, the civilization of the world; the perfect development of the human reason and its attainment to universal command over individualism; the apotheosis of man (man becoming God)."[13] Believing the state to be divine, Progressives naturally thought of state power as being unlimited. Don't take my word for it, take Burgess's; the state's highest priority, he said, was achieving "the original, absolute, unlimited, universal power over the individual subject, and all associations of subjects."[14]

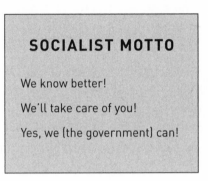

SOCIALIST MOTTO

We know better!

We'll take care of you!

Yes, we (the government) can!

Scoffing at biblical concepts like "fixed truths" and "permanent principles," Progressives looked at faith-based groups, churches, and private associations as troublesome entities that misdirected citizens' attention from statist ideals to individual responsibilities. Belief in bureaucratic experts? Yes! Belief in Progressive leadership? Yes! Belief in government know how? Yes! Belief in government action? Yes! Belief in God or the individual? Not so much.

Woodrow Wilson, a firm believer in Progressivism, described government in near-mystical terms. "Government," he declared, "is not a machine, but a living thing. It falls, not under the theory of the universe, but under the theory of organic life. It is accountable to Darwin, not to Newton."[15]

The clear shift from proven virtues to experimental values, and from permanent principles to progressive programs, was a low blow to the Founders' principle-driven philosophy. Thomas Jefferson wrote, "I think we have more machinery of government than is necessary, too many parasites living on the labor of the industrious."[16] It's hard to believe he'd approve of the Progressives' demand for an ever-growing government.

Elite Administrators Trump Citizen Legislators

The Founders believed in citizen legislators, that laws should be made by wise, experienced, and virtuous elected officials with roots in local communities. Viewing this notion as amateurish, Progressives considered politics too complex for common folks. They believed government responsibilities should be stripped from local yokels, given to "experts," and administered through agencies controlled by a centralized power base.[17]

According to Dr. Ron Prostritto, "The idea of separating politics and administration—of grounding a significant portion of government not on the basis of popular consent but on expertise—was a fundamental aim of American Progressivism that explains the Progressives' fierce assault on the Founders' separation-of-powers constitutionalism."[18]

The Progressives were greatly assisted by the ratification of two Constitutional amendments in 1913. The first, the Sixteenth Amendment, legalized the federal income tax, which began at a modest rate of 1 percent. At the time, politicians assured the citizens the income tax rate would never grow more than a few percentage points. I guess it all depends on your definition of "a few"—is it really any surprise that federal income tax rates now range up to 35 percent, and that much higher rates look likely in the near future, especially for the successful? This is the nature of government—it always seeks to expand its size, power, and resources. The income tax profoundly changed the nature of American government, creating the means for government to grow exponentially bigger than anything our Founders had contemplated. And yet, with all this money, the government still can't pay its bills.

The second transformational act was the Seventeenth Amendment, which provided for the direct election of U.S. senators. This change denied state legislatures, which had previously selected senators, the power to protect state and municipal governments against federal overreach and encroachment. It overturned a crucial check on the federal government's power that had been carefully thought out by the Founders.

Progressives exploited these amendments to erode our fundamental principles. Thus, individualism, self-governance, and Godliness were being chipped away even before the War on Success came along and tried to finish them off. For Progressives, expanding government was not a means to an end, but an end in itself. Their movement was extremely influential, setting the model for socialist activism in America to this day. It is no coincidence that Obama's followers often call themselves "Progressives"—the original Progressives are the key inspiration for today's would-be social engineers.

SOCIAL DEMOCRACY:
SECOND TRIMESTER SOCIALISM

Advocates of American socialism can't point to the Soviet Union anymore as their inspiration, since socialism failed so spectacularly there. Socialism in other states such as China and Vietnam has proved so inept that the Communist rulers themselves are moving toward capitalism—so they're not good role models either. Instead, we're told that we should strive to emulate European "Social Democracies."

The term "Social Democracy" sounds disarming enough unless you understand that the "social" part means socialism. Social Democracy is just a lighter, softer socialism. Think of it as second trimester socialism—she is just starting to show. This is the creeping, "polite-sounding" socialism that gradually invades a capitalist society through progressively more government intervention in the private sector, expanding welfare schemes, and ever-growing regulations for individual citizens. Sound familiar?

More subtle than Communism, Social Democracies substitute excessive regulations for formal state control of commerce Think of Social Democracy as socialism without the marching, the bloodshed, and the missile parades. It doesn't leave us dead in the street, but dead on the inside without our big dreams, lofty ambitions, or our distinctive identities.

Social Democracy is time-released economic suicide. It feels like an overbearing mother-in-law, constantly nagging you, but with the force of law. Steadily, the need for community service, churches, private charities, and interpersonal generosity is minimized, as the government tries to ensure "equality" by reducing the ability and desire to become wealthy, and by assuming all responsibility for caring for the poor. The writer Victor Davis Hanson notes that living in a Social Democracy is "like running in a race where the goal is that all the runners cross the finish line at the same time, corner-eyes fixed on each other, scared to death that some trouble-maker might try to bolt out ahead."[19]

Instead of revolution, Social Democracies emerge gradually through evolution. This is the "boiling frog" approach. No smart frog would stay in a pot of boiling water. But if you put the frog in cold water and gradually turn up the heat, the frog will become accustomed to the change until it's too late and he's cooked. We see this progression in America today, as many Americans tolerate rising taxes, more regulations, and more intrusive government without consciously realizing where all this is leading. As the novelist C. S. Lewis warned, "The safest road to Hell is the gradual one—the gentle slope, soft underfoot, without sudden turning, without milestones, without signposts."[20]

THE UNITED STATES OF EURMERICA?

Europe is the quintessential Social Democracy, the model that our administration wants to emulate. So let's look at the kinds of policies we find in European nations.

Consistent with human nature, the European experience shows that social programs that reward individuals for not working are amazingly successful at keeping people from working. Surprised? And those who have jobs don't work very much. French workers are *legally required* to take at least five weeks of vacation time per year, and many go ahead and take off eight weeks. Mind you, they also enjoy twelve paid holidays and a 35-hour work week. And if you work your way up into the top tiers in France, your income is taxed at 60 percent.[21]

We find a similar situation in Germany, where workers also play by a 35-hour-a-week rule and enjoy six weeks of paid vacation. What's more, German welfare benefits account for 48 percent of the federal budget. With such generous benefits, it's no surprise that in Europe overall, more than 20 percent of the working-age population depends on welfare for their primary income.[22] And here's an arresting statistic: since 1970, all of Europe has added 4 million jobs, while the United States has created 57 million jobs during the same time span.[23]

Sweden provides a good case study. In that country, even after "reforms," government unemployment benefits amount to 80 percent of a person's salary for 200 days, then 70 percent for another 100 days, and 65 percent for the next 150 days. And parents have eighteen months for maternity or paternity leave at virtually full salary. As reported in *The Sunday Times*, "Sweden's workers are highly paid yet heavily taxed, and they support a younger generation of people who are unemployed but drawing generous benefits.[24]

Despite such government "care," however, 20 percent of Swedes complain of anxiety syndromes such as depression, burnout, and panic attacks. As Dr. David Eberhard, chief psychiatrist at Stockholm's St. Goran's Hospital, said, "We are actually the safest country in the world...but people are feeling psychologically worse and worse." It's hard to tell, though, how many Swedes really are depressed, and how many just say they are to suck benefits out of the government. As reported in the *Wall Street Journal*, for several years, hundreds of Swedes were diagnosed with "electro-hypersensitivity"—that is, an allergy to electricity— and awarded state-funded sick pay worth 80 percent of their salary. The Swedish system has encouraged its citizens to turn life's difficulties into clinical issues.

Assar Lindbeck, a noted Swedish economist, says the lenient welfare state has "changed" the country over the last generation, replacing the old Protestant work ethic and making it much more acceptable to live off government benefits. Lindbeck added, "I would not call it cheating. I would call it a drift in attitudes and social norms."[25] Nice euphemism—perhaps he's the one that named Obama's wasteful $787 billion spending bill the "American Reinvestment & Recovery Act."

According to a report in the *Financial Times*, "Europe is a continent of high and persistent unemployment, declining productivity growth, rapid aging and growing fiscal strains. . . . Its high taxes and benefits discourage anybody form doing too well, while ensuring that nobody does badly."[26]

Europeans don't work particularly hard, because they don't want to navigate through all the red tape to start or expand businesses. Besides, their success will be exorbitantly taxed, and the government will take care of them anyway, whether they work hard or not. Consider the recent French book, *Bonjour Laziness*, which advises people on how to get by with the minimum amount of work.[27] The author, who is a part-time government worker, explains, "The aim is to keep your job without working. It's not to go higher."[28] I'd feel a lot better about the French work ethic if this book hadn't become a runaway bestseller.

Here in America, if we keep up the current pace of hope and change, we won't have to travel abroad to see Social Democracy. It will be right here, in our own back yard. But the warning signs are being ignored. Americans still associate socialism with bloody revolutions. This misperception has lulled us into a false sense of complacency. Too many citizens think, "This could never happen to us." On guard against gun-bearing militants marching under red flags, they don't notice the insidious spread of European-style socialist policies, and especially the socialist mentality.

Here is the choice: we can renew our self-motivated first principles of limited government, merit, free thinking, and a self-reliant citizenry, or we can join Europe and most other Western countries on their path to self-destruction.

Let's rethink the European Dream.

THE FALL OF ROME—
AND LONDON, PARIS, BERLIN . . .

Now that we understand the policies and mindset of Social Democracy, let's consider the results this system has achieved.

The European Union is like a massive welfare state characterized by huge financial transfers from the most productive to the least productive sectors. If you go there, you see lots of identical-looking little cars, apartments, and houses. There's a lot of sameness in Europe.

Here's a quick quiz. In less than ten seconds, can you name the last exciting or helpful breakthrough that has come out of Western Europe? In fact, see if you can name any. Consider medicine, pharmaceuticals, the arts, technology, manufacturing, athletics, and any other category of human accomplishment. The list of notable achievements coming out of Europe in the last four decades should embarrass even the most committed socialist.

Europe, sadly, is declining rapidly, possibly even dying—the birthrate of many European states is so low that they have to import a new tax base from the Middle East. The connection between more socialism and less children is quite logical—why

RECENT CONTRIBUTIONS OF EUROPEAN SOCIAL DEMOCRACY

This page left intentionally blank

bother having children when you can't earn a surplus to take care of them or achieve a legacy to leave behind for them?

There is, however, one group in Europe that still shows exceptional initiative, risk-taking, and energy—the rising numbers of disillusioned Europeans who are leaving the sameness and achievement ceilings behind and immigrating here. These are the real gems, like our earliest settlers and the throngs of immigrants who followed them. They come to America looking for nothing but opportunity. Those who have lived with socialism seem to love freedom even more than those of us who've had freedom all our life. This is also true for hard-working, opportunity-seeking immigrants from across the globe.

And what do Europeans themselves say about their long experience living under Social Democracy? They're voting against it. In the French election of 2007, Socialist Ségolène Royal was defeated by conservative-leaning Nicolas Sarkozy, who campaigned on the decidedly anti-socialist platform of restoring the work ethic and cutting welfare. In Germany, Chancellor Angela Merkel's Christian Democrats were re-elected in September 2009, with the Social Democrats suffering the biggest loss of any party in modern German history. And in Britain, polls project the ruling leftwing Labor Party will lose power to the Conservatives in the election expected next year.

Overall, thanks to this supposedly gentle brand of socialism, Europe is lost, preoccupying itself with its grand history as an escape from its grim future. America, in contrast, is future-focused. We are still making history and will continue to do so— but we must jump off the track to socialism.

Not surprisingly, almost every European who I interviewed for this book raised the same question: "Why is America moving in our direction when it hasn't worked for us and we want to be more like you?" It's a question worth considering. Many Americans are completely in the dark when it comes to the

meaning of "Social Democracy," especially the college-age generation. After all, "social" sounds like fun with friends and family,
and "democracy" sounds like freedom. But when you put those
terms together, you get a system dramatically different from the
system of free enterprise and limited government that our
Founders created.

For decades, we have traveled to Europe to explore history. If
we don't change course, however, we'll be going there to get a
glimpse of our future.

KINDRED SPIRITS

From all outward appearances, the Obama administration is seeking to throw together an Americanized version of Social Democracy. But Obama knows he can't explicitly proclaim his socialist
intentions, so he resorts to thinly veiled code words about "fixing," "transforming," and "re-making" America.

European socialists, of course, are thrilled to have an American
president join their ranks. The Norwegians even thought Obama's
intentions were worthy of a Nobel Prize—and to be sure, nothing
epitomizes the socialist mindset more than passing out rewards for
good intentions. Of course, Obama has a special attraction for
European socialists, since his economic policies will drag the
American economy down toward European levels. And that
makes the world more "fair," in European eyes.

European socialists want to spread socialism internationally, or
wealth and power will flow to those nations that retain economic
freedom. Europe has slowly recognized that socialism doesn't
work so well when their businesses can just hop across the pond
and participate in a free market. As best-selling author Dick Morris points out, Europe loves Obama for "disciplining the unruly
United States and taming it to be a member of the European family of nations."[29] That much is clear. Why Obama loves Europe...
that's more of a mystery.

WHO SUPPORTS SOCIALISM?

With its miserable track record, how could the delusion of socialistic utopia still be alive in 2010? First off, we should acknowledge that many well-meaning individuals genuinely believe that socialism helps the needy. They are wrong, of course, and even a cursory look at the extreme poverty and absence of hope that characterized the entire Eastern Bloc, from the Soviet Union to East Germany, should really disabuse everyone of the notion that socialism works. But some people inexplicably believe in it anyway, and we need to offer such folks a crash course in the principles and practices of the free market.

Quite simply, the enduring appeal of socialism boils down to human nature. As human beings, we tend to continue doing things both individually and collectively that are detrimental to us. We continue spending despite our debt. We continue overeating despite being overweight. We keep treating our spouse the same way when the relationship isn't working. We know the higher path, yet too frequently choose the lower. Doing the same thing but expecting different results is commonly referred to as the insanity cycle.

In many instances, we even acknowledge our error but continue repeating the same mistake nonetheless. Understanding the weaknesses of human nature, our Founders structured the Constitution to disperse power, not to micro-manage every decision or to address every imagined grievance. As Lord Acton famously put it, "Power corrupts and absolute power corrupts absolutely."

All of us share culpability for allowing the seeds of socialism to grow. But at the risk of sounding like a counterrevolutionary, I will highlight a handful of enablers who deserve extra attention.

Parents and Grandparents

First and foremost, and maybe surprisingly, too many parents and grandparents have abdicated to our educational institutions, and to modern society at large, the teaching of American history, free-market philosophy, and the founding principles of this nation. But that's not what schools teach anymore. When kids don't learn these values at home, the destructive influence of the socialist-minded mass media, Hollywood elites, and teachers' unions fills the void.

The Clergy

Ignoring the horrors of socialism and blind to the lessons of history, many well-meaning but seriously misguided pastors and preachers have expressed direct or indirect support for socialist policies and denied the opposing, clear-cut principles of the Bible. Succumbing to the affecting arguments favoring the cold hand of state-based compassion, these religious leaders have sacrificed their scriptural integrity for the false hope and hollow promises of a counterfeit Eden.

Clearly, like all of us, clergymen are susceptible to conforming to the material world rather than being transformed by the spiritual renewal of their minds. But the clergy must strive to teach the authentic principles of truth no matter the personal cost. Socialism denies absolute truth, permanent principles, and in most cases a living God. It's time for pastors, priests, and rabbis to take a stand and repudiate this anti-biblical ideology. How can you continue to play both sides of this clearly defined fence?

The Media

Our biggest newspapers and network news programs hardly even pretend to be objective anymore. By selectively covering or not covering certain stories, by strategically writing headlines to support their candidate, by happily running unverified stories, by collaborating on White House public relation campaigns, and by abolishing the distinction between news and commentary, the mainstream media have turned into what many call the "state run media," however unofficial that title may be for now. The media's subjective, biased, and unprofessional news coverage has undermined and suppressed the free flow of information that is vital to a free citizenry.

For a socialist government to retain power, it must directly or indirectly control the flow of ideas. Despite the Obama administration's lock on the mainstream media, dissenting ideas are still bubbling to the surface, especially through talk radio. That's why talk radio is the target of a concerted attempt to reinstate the Fairness Doctrine—an FCC regulation whose abolition under President Reagan provided the spark for today's talk radio renaissance.

Fifty-two percent of journalists acknowledge they voted for John Kerry in the 2004 election,[30] and less than 10 percent report being conservative.[31] Nonetheless, reporters claim their professionalism overrides their bias. Americans, however, don't believe them; 51 percent of voters think the press helped Obama win election, while just 7 percent believe they favored John McCain. Overall, nearly 70 percent of Americans believe news organizations are politically biased and that reporters try to help their candidate win.[32]

Our Educators

Teachers, administrators, and textbook publishers have immense power in shaping the minds of our children. Unfortunately, they misuse this power to indoctrinate our children and grandchildren with socialist propaganda, emphasizing America's mistakes over its greatness, social justice over the three R's, political correctness over historical accuracy, and affective learning over critical thinking. The hearts and minds of upcoming generations are being trained to expect the government to usher in a new socialist paradise.

Since the government runs most of our schools, it has a vested interest in teaching children that government is good. Is it any wonder that this system for decades has produced millions of barely capable adults looking to government for their subsistence? Many of our educational institutions have become nothing more than breeding grounds for a unionized and subsidized adulthood. Despite the best effort of many dedicated teachers, the system often gobbles up a student and spits out a government dependent.

Hollywood

It's no surprise that those who live and breathe in the land of make-believe are really big fans of really big government, flaunting their celebrity status to promote the hip causes and trendy utopian ideals of the day. From its 1940s-era infatuation with Marxism to its worship of Al Gore and mother earth today, Tinseltown knows how to tug the right emotional strings and sway a generation one screen at a time.

Oscar-winning filmmaker Michael Moore defined capitalism as "legalized greed" in his recent "documentary," *Capitalism: A Love Story*. (I wonder if he'll condemn his own profits from that film as "legalized greed.") Oblivious to the concept of service and value that drive the free market and blind to the law of sowing and reaping, his attitude is quite common to clueless Hollywood stars pretending to be political geniuses.

Ironically, most Hollywood celebrities are themselves products of American exceptionalism. They worked hard, persisted doggedly, and eventually triumphed. Most of us admire them for achieving the American Dream. Like Obama, however, they don't think anyone else can do it. They tend to cultivate an elite, condescending mentality, believing themselves to be more enlightened than the hoi polloi. Considering the astounding rate of drug abuse, eating disorders, and divorce in Hollywood, one wonders what exactly they really can teach the rest of us.

The Democratic Party

On the national political stage, socialism is largely advanced through the Democratic Party, with the Obama administration providing the primary example. The U.S. Senate includes one openly socialist member, Vermont's Bernie Sanders, who predictably caucuses with the Democratic Party and is counted as a Democrat for the purposes of committee assignments. The House of Representatives is home to a slew of semi-closeted socialists who belong to one or more radical House organizations including the Progressive Democrats of America (six members), the Congressional Progressive Caucus (seventy-four members), and the Congressional Black Caucus (forty-three House members).[33] There is also the avowedly socialist Democratic Socialists of America, which has loose ties with the Democrats.

The Democrats' turn toward socialism was heralded decades ago by Norman Thomas, a former leader of the Socialist Party of America. Ronald Reagan liked to quote Thomas's chilling diagnosis: "The American people would never vote for socialism. But...under the name of 'liberalism' the American people will adopt every fragment of the socialist program."[34]

In addition to all the above categories of enablers, a few others deserve a dishonorable mention:

1. *Academics*: Insulated by tenure from the need to produce anything of value, college professors have a lot of time to dream up grand schemes for re-engineering society—and to teach these to captive students.
2. *The Guilty Rich*: Some successful people feel guilty about their wealth and seek to ease their consciences by

supporting socialist policies. This group is distinct from the ambitious, affluent entrepreneurial segment, or what I call "the working rich."

3. *The Lazy and Lethargic*: No explanation is needed for this politically incorrect but real-life category.

4. *The Faithless*: Some atheists look to big government to answer their prayers without the hassle and inconvenience of formal religious ceremonies.

5. *Leaders Who Amass Great Power*: This does not yet apply to America, but many foreign leaders have promised to deliver a socialist paradise. Interestingly, not a single leader has ever claimed to have created Utopia and then stepped aside, their work complete. One can see the attraction of being an all-powerful socialist leader, though personally, I'd probably be overthrown for giving the money back to the people who earned it.

SOCIALISM IN THE CLASSROOM

Dr. Michael Youssef is the founder and president of *Leading the Way with Dr. Michael Youssef,* a wordwide ministry whose broadcasts reach more than a billion people. Dr. Youssef once told me a story that illustrated simply and clearly how socialism kills success. The story was about a Texas Tech economics professor who once failed his entire class. Here's how it happened. After listening to his students argue vociferously that socialism creates a fairer, more just society, the professor tried an experiment. He announced that test grades henceforth would be determined by averaging all the students' grades—in other words, every student would get the same grade.

The class averaged a low "B" on the first test. The result disappointed a handful of students who had studied hard and thought they had earned an "A," but others who didn't study at all were quite pleased. On the next test, the class average dropped by a steep twelve points to a low "C." This severely upset the good students, sparking tension between them and the students who didn't study.

The class average sunk to a "D" on the next test, angering even the worst students, who had grown accustomed to "B's" and "C's." The high-achieving students became so disengaged that they largely skipped the last two weeks of class. Thus, no one was surprised when the class flunked the final exam.

In the end, despite the poor grades, the students learned a good lesson: *When you try to prevent failure, no one really succeeds. When you try to make everyone a winner, you just create more losers.*

THE REMAKING OF AMERICA

Looking across the socialist utopias scattered throughout Europe today, you hardly ever see the attitude that gives rise to excellence. We've seen that attitude a lot in American history. We saw it in our Founding Fathers; in Carnegie's drive to earn millions and then give it all away; in Edison's 5,000 plus tries; in Kennedy's ambition for the moon; in Martin Luther King's big dream; in Neil Armstrong's giant leap for mankind; in Reagan's call to tear down the Berlin Wall; in Bill Gates's struggle to put a computer on every desk; in Lance Armstrong's triumph over cancer and seven-time victory in the Tour de France; in Tiger Woods's dominance on the golf course; in the counterattack on Flight 93; and in the patriotism of 9/12. This is the American spirit, and this is what's at risk.

Look at it another way. There are two segments of the American population: those who want to take care of themselves, and those who wish to be taken care of like a ward of the state. Put another way, there are those who want to grow up, and those who want to defer adulthood and functionally remain children.

We must fix the dysfunctional relationship between the individual and the state, and do so quickly.

On the continuum of success, socialism has been somewhere between a big disappointment and a tragedy everywhere it has been tried. Why would we ever go down this path? But should we choose to do so, as Victor Davis Hanson put it, "More of us will soon be working for the government, habitually striking, hunting out that rare capitalist in hiding for a shake-down, and bitching over our weary 35 hour work week."[35]

It may be kind and gentle, but it's socialism all the same.

CHAPTER SEVEN

GOD IS NOT A SOCIALIST

"Socialism is a philosophy of failure, the creed of ignorance, and the gospel of envy; its inherent virtue is the equal sharing of misery."

—WINSTON CHURCHILL

SOCIALIZATION IS ALWAYS ACCOMPANIED by secularization—the smaller God becomes, the larger government grows. Of course, that's a human perspective; God doesn't shrink at all. But as God fades from our attention, so does liberty. Evil in all its varieties is just the natural outgrowth of freedom without God. Review the whole history of godless Communism and fascism—did anything good come of it?

No doubt about it, America's system of free enterprise, like our founding documents, is inspired by the timeless truths revealed throughout the Old and New Testaments. But today, the diminishing of God has led Americans to feel lonely, confused, and isolated like never before. Disconnected from traditional and proven sources of value and love, more and more people now seek solace in government programs. The result has been a decline in individual freedom and the diminishing of our range of lifetime opportunities.

This is the inevitable result when a country moves toward socialism. The socialist deplores biblical absolutes or fixed truths of any kind, for they restrict his ability to manipulate feelings and influence the masses. Communist godfather Karl Marx was a philosophical materialist, meaning he didn't believe in God or any spiritual realm. To Marx, if you couldn't see it, it didn't exist: the material world is all there is. This warped atheism is a crucial component of the socialist mindset, justifying their attempts to create a utopian "workers' paradise" on earth.

Nevertheless, today's socialists deceptively weave biblical quotes and spiritual-sounding platitudes into their rhetoric to help win over the "innocently ignorant" people of faith. American socialists are particularly prone to selling their ideology in religious terms. After all, our nation was founded on biblical principles, and according to recent polls, 80 percent of Americans claim to believe in God, and 77 percent profess to be either Christian or Jewish.[1] Socialists can't explicitly reject God and expect to win election, so instead they try to co-opt Him as a salesman for their atheistic cause.

Because they don't really believe in God, many socialists are biblically illiterate, despite their biblical sales pitch. They twist God's instructions and the values He extols, extracting collectivist lessons where none exist. Unfortunately, many religious people, congregants and leaders alike, who recognize these distortions are reluctant to challenge them, either because they're intimidated by political correctness or because they don't fully understand the harsh reality of socialism.

Although the socialist claims to be doing God's work, the big, cold hand of the federal government is no match for the warm, loving hands of God. Socialism does not produce spiritual fulfillment anywhere, and it never brings man closer to God.

IT'S ALL ABOUT HUMAN NATURE

Contrary to the appeals of socialists, their ideology is incompatible with both the letter and the spirit of the Bible. To understand why, one must understand the truth of God and the biblical worldview that naturally follows. The Bible teaches that God is all-loving, all-powerful, all-knowing, merciful, just, and unchanging. God knows everything about us and loves us anyway. God cares for us, cheers for us, and wants the best for us. The apostle Paul presents a beautiful description of God and the things of God as lovely, pure, true, gracious, just, excellent, and worthy of praise (Philippians 4:8).

We can begin to understand God by looking at the beginning, the beginning of everything. The first chapter of Genesis shows that God was well-pleased with each act of creation. And, after He put the final touches on the sixth day, God looked upon the universe and all He had made and proclaimed that "indeed it was very good."[2]

The original entrepreneur and innovator of the universe had established the model of productivity and excellence to be emulated by all humanity. God took special delight in His priority creation of man and woman. How do we know? Well, He made us in His image and likeness as individual souls so that we could mirror His nature. Moreover, our Creator granted us authority over all living things, blessed us, and charged us with filling the earth with our offspring.[3]

For a while, everything was blissful. Then Adam and Eve gave in to temptation, willfully broke God's law, and ate from the forbidden tree (Genesis 3:6). That changed everything, corrupting the nature of mankind.[4] Ever since the Fall of Man, all men and women have had to deal with instinctive but counterproductive character traits. In fact, blaming was introduced to the world simultaneously by Adam, who pointed the finger at Eve, and Eve, who blamed the devil.[5]

Human nature has not changed since then. We come from the factory with standard flaws in our moral fiber such as laziness, selfishness, greed, ignorance, and vanity, to name a few. These traits can be mitigated or even leveraged for good, but we cannot eliminate them. We succeed in life if we develop enough virtue to override those vices. And society can assist our success by establishing rewards for the behaviors that we want repeated and penalties for behaviors we want diminished.

In opposition to the Biblical view, socialists think human nature can change. They believe people are intrinsically neither good nor bad, but simply the products of their environment. Thus, people who commit crimes or otherwise misbehave are excused as victims of capitalism, poverty, racism, sexism, bad parenting, and other ills that supposedly plague our society. Socialists believe that human nature is plastic and can be twisted, fashioned, shaped, and molded by an improved environment. They suggest that

SOCIALISM VS. THE BIBLE

1. Socialism is about taking.
   The Bible is about giving.

2. Socialism is about dependence on government.
   The Bible is about dependence on God.

3. Socialism is rooted in fear.
   The Bible is rooted in faith.

4. Socialism promotes sameness.
   The Bible promotes uniqueness.

5. Socialism produces mediocrity.
   The Bible produces excellence.

6. Socialism hides the truth.
   The Bible reveals the truth.

7. Socialism restricts free will.
   The Bible creates free will.

8. Socialism changes the symptom.
   The Bible changes the source.

9. Socialism elevates politicians.
   The Bible elevates God's children.

10. Socialism has never worked.
    The Bible has never failed.

human nature would improve if only society could be restructured with the perfect recipe of ingredients for paradise and delight.

In practice, for socialists, "improving a person's environment" means providing him with property or other goods that were taken from someone who earned them. This caters to the downside of human nature—envy, greed, and laziness—while suppressing the upside—hard work and self-reliance. The socialists' notion that this tactic, if repeated on a large enough scale, will ultimately elevate human nature, is of course absurd. Conveniently, however, this tactic also solidifies the socialists' power base, comprising a growing number of people who rely on their benevolence. So we're left to wonder whether socialists really believe in their own ideology, or if it's just a good pretext for expanding their power.

OUR FATHER WHO ART IN HEAVEN

So that we could better grasp His love for us and the cherished connection He desires to have with us, God established the father-child relationship theme beginning in Genesis and running throughout the Bible. To fully appreciate the incompatibility of socialism with biblical truth, we should understand how this spiritual metaphor reinforces our correct standing with God.

There are many ways we can imitate our heavenly father. We imitate God when we tell the truth, when we act in love, when we show grace, when we are faithful to our spouses, when we are wise stewards of our resources, when we are industrious, when we demonstrate faith, and so on. When we copy God's ways, we reflect His character in our lives. As the apostle Paul said, "Be imitators of God, therefore, as dearly loved children" (Ephesians 5:1).

We imitate God when we are productive human beings, when we employ our natural gifts, and when we encourage others, especially our children, to do likewise. When God created you and me, He planted within us the instinct and drive to work, invent, produce, create, and own, because in doing so, we imitate Him, assign credit to Him, and further His creation.

A natural validation of biblical truth, capitalism brings out all these qualities of character that God wants to develop within us. To succeed in the free market, we have to be creative, industrious, self-reliant, frugal, and resourceful. Whether we are a small business owner, plumber, banker, or chief executive, capitalism is all about learning from our mistakes, overcoming fear, and serving others in ways that are desired, appreciated, and rewarded. Developing these character traits mimics God and honors His acts of creation.

God made us with free will, with the insatiable appetite for freedom, for designing our lives to fit our individual dreams. And this is what inspired the Founders of our country. They wanted to create a government that is most in line with God's creation, most in line with rewarding and enhancing the positive aspects of human nature that lead to productive behavior. As historian Johan Norberg wrote, "Believing in capitalism does not mean believing in growth, the economy, or efficiency. Desirable as they may be, those are only the results. At its core, belief in capitalism is belief in mankind."[6]

On nearly every level, socialism violates all the positive character traits God gave us to develop. Independent thinking and entrepreneurial innovation are suppressed because they inhibit central planning, Instead of filling us with exhortations toward self-improvement, socialists preach victimization and government dependence. In socialism, the drive to improve, succeed, and prosper must be checked at the gate for the sake of the greater good. But the greater good is no substitute for the greater God.

Despite their philanthropic public persona, socialists relish the idea of being in charge of a nation's wealth. Promoted under a shroud of selflessness, "show me the money" remains their battle cry. Socialist-leaning governments tend to think of themselves, not God, as the source of individual rights, and therefore see nothing wrong with taking one person's property and deeding it to another.

Far from being biblically inspired, socialists regard God as their biggest rival, even bigger than capitalism. Among other things, the Bible instructs private citizens to be wise, responsible, industrious, excellent, thrifty, charitable, debt-free, and optimistic. As you see, these habits of virtue conflict with the priorities of the socialist state. If citizens depend on God and become self-reliant, socialism loses its allure. To prevent God from stealing their thunder, so to speak, socialists work either outwardly or covertly to minimize the influence of God in culture and especially in public life.

BIBLICAL GIVING VS. SOCIALIST TAKING

To understand the spirit of God, we must study the word of God. There is no shortcut. And in examining the scripture, we see the stark contrast between socialism and the Bible can be articulated in just nine words:

The Bible is about giving. Socialism is about taking.

This is simple, direct, and doesn't require scholarly understanding. For example, in the New Testament, we are reminded of the giving principle, that our giving determines our getting. Jesus said, "Give, and it will be given to you. A good measure, pressed down, shaken together and running over, will be poured into your lap. For with the measure you use, it will be measured to you" (Luke 6:38). In other words, similar to the ACORN voting method, we should give early and give often. There is no mention of stealing, expropriating, or redistributing of any sort.

Despite its hopey-changey veneer, socialism poses this central question: *"How could I get more?"* The socialist doesn't believe in giving, he believes in *taking*. For the socialist, Jesus' teaching transforms into something different: *"Take from others and you shall have plenty. For the more you take, the more you will be able to keep."*

Socialist politicians ask, "How can we get more cash from the successful?" And irresponsible citizens ask, "How can we get more for ourselves without contributing more?" Turning President Kennedy's words upside down, too many Americans seem to be asking not what they can do for their country, but what their country can do for them. Or more precisely, *what their favorite politicians can give them.*

Wise politicians ask, "How can we encourage citizens to generously give more time, more resources, and more service?" And responsible citizens ask, "How can I increase my service and contribution to others?" This, incidentally, is also the question that guides entrepreneurs. The super-successful raise the bar even higher and ask, "How could I go the extra mile? How could I over-deliver and give much more than my customers expect?" As the great personal success advocate Napoleon Hill wrote, "In every soul there has been deposited the seed of a great future, but that seed will never germinate, much less grow to maturity, except through the rendering of useful service."[7]

The Bible *never* advocates taking from one person for the purpose of giving to another. This is a manmade, spiritually corrupt concoction. St. Francis of Assisi said, "For it is in giving that we receive," and Maya Angelou added, "I have found that among its other benefits, giving liberates the soul of the giver." Note the emphasis on giving, not taking and redistributing.

Reflect upon the Golden Rule for a moment: "So in everything, do to others what you would have them do to you, for this sums up the Law and the Prophets" (Matthew 7:12). If we use this biblical maxim as a gauge for personal decisions and public policy, the light of truth shines ever so brightly. If we don't want someone to kick us in the shin, then we don't kick them in the shin. If we don't want others to take from us, how could we ever condone, encourage, or promote taking from others?

Think of it this way: the *faithful* focus on giving. The *fearful* focus on taking.

SOCIALISM VIOLATES SOWING & REAPING

The principle of the harvest states that we will reap what we have sown. The Bible says, "The point is this; he who sows sparingly will also reap sparingly; and he who sows bountifully will also reap bountifully" (2 Corinthians 9:6). This is a wonderful promise reminding us that the actions we take today create the world we live in tomorrow.

Socialism breaches this law by forcefully expropriating the fruit of people's labor and transferring it to others. One citizen gets what he *didn't plant* and another citizen doesn't get what he *did plant*. (And the course of redistribution, of course, includes a generous "processing and handling fee" for the government bureaucrat.)

During moments of weakness, we've all probably wished for a socialist version of the sowing and reaping maxim. But I double checked the ancient scriptures and couldn't find anything close. The apostle Paul was emphatic about this: "Do not be deceived, God is not mocked; for whatever a man sows, that he will also reap" (Galatians 6:7).

Obviously, we don't imitate God when we steal or accept stolen goods. In the Eighth Commandment, God makes this clear in four words: "Thou shall not steal." This Commandment clearly condemns expropriation, and Leviticus lays out an entire system for dealing with those who steal.[8] Similarly, the Tenth Commandment says, "Do Not Covet" (Exodus 20:17), which in and of itself repudiates the entire underpinnings of socialism. And remember, these are Commandments, not suggestions.

Socialists often cite biblical imperatives to generosity, but God would never make us break His own Commandments in order to be "generous." And besides, expropriation is not generosity at all, it's simply theft.

The principle of the harvest is intended to encourage us to make wise decisions: if we don't study today, and then we flunk our physics test tomorrow, it's not because God is punishing us, nor does it make us a victim. We just didn't follow His principles. This is part of God's design, intended to encourage wise decisions. And God doesn't recommend that the government give us someone else's harvest—He wants us to responsibly plan for our own future.

From a practical standpoint, if we have something we haven't earned, we often don't get to keep it anyway. Sooner or later, people tend to get separated from dishonest or easy gain. Lottery winners often go broke within a few years of their windfall. Get-rich-quick attempts usually backfire. Of course, common thieves don't typically invest their money wisely, which is why they steal again and again.

There is, of course, a cosmic justice in all this. God wants us to work hard and earn our own keep. And as in all things in life, good things tend to happen to those who listen to Him.

FALSE COMPASSION

Redistribution is not endorsed in scripture. To the contrary, the Bible expressly rejects the notion of preferential treatment—for the poor or the rich—with this teaching from Moses: "Do not pervert justice; do not show partiality to the poor or favoritism to the great, but judge your neighbor fairly" (Leviticus 19:15). Let's think of this as the original, premium standard of fairness. Both sides treated without preference—what a concept! Understand, though, that socialists habitually blur the distinction between public justice and private compassion.

From Genesis to Revelation, the Bible advocates generosity and compassion toward the poor and the hungry—but this is a *private* matter. It's a personal duty, not a government mandate. This is not callousness; rather, it reveals God's wisdom in knowing the inevitable abuse and exploitation that would result from expropriations. And all sorts of other ills arise from turning God's love for all his children into divisive political pandering. This is not "hope," nor is it the path to positive "change."

Socialism claims a monopoly on compassion, but it's really a counterfeit compassion, a cruel knock off of the real deal that creates far more ills than it repairs. Socialism is not compassion; it's blunt force. And history proves that the short-term, expedient fix that socialism may supply is far outweighed by the unhealthy, long-term addiction it causes. Furthermore, government-enforced "giving" robs the citizen of the spiritual joys that come from freely giving of one's self and one's resources, while infusing the recipient with a warped sense of entitlement.

While the Founders had soft hearts for the needy, they didn't want the federal government in the welfare business. They believed family, friends, churches, charities, and if necessary, local governments should fill the role, but not the federal government which, they foresaw, would get carried away playing God. And they were right.

IN GOVERNMENT WE TRUST

The Bible teaches that God loves us as individuals. He made each of us a purpose-filled, unique work of art—an unrepeatable miracle, each with a different gift to deliver to the world. It's the same attitude we, as parents, have toward our own children—each child is priceless and irreplaceable.

Socialists, however, don't trust the individual. Independent-thinking, self-reliant citizens are a real thorn in their side. They don't like dissent either, as individuals are expected to yield their hopes and dreams for the sake of the collective good. They believe individual rights are conferred by the government to its subjects, not by God to His children. In fact, the only group that socialists regard as having individual merit is socialist politicians. Because they are ostensibly bringing us a socialist paradise, their own fortunes become synonymous with the "greater good."

As the instrument for bringing about a socialist society, the federal government is upheld by the socialist as the closest thing to heaven on earth. It offers glory, power, prestige, other people's money—all the things socialist leaders expect to be waiting for them just beyond the pearly gates, but without the delay, suspense, or inconvenience of death. Believing they are surrogates for the one, true God, socialists worship themselves instead of their Creator. With their exaltation of government, socialists pull citizens' devotion away from God and toward the government.

Consider the very first line of the Founders' greatest achievement, the United States Constitution. It begins with "We the people...." That in itself conveys the entire point of the document.

In contrast, consider the opening of Saul Alinsky's *Rules for Radicals*: "What follows is for those who want to change the world from what it is to what they believe it should be. *The Prince* was written by Machiavelli for the Haves on how to hold power. *Rules for Radicals* is written for the Have-Nots on how to take it away."[9] Likewise, the *Communist Manifesto* begins, "The history of all hitherto existing societies is the history of class struggles"— a fitting start to a tome advocating class warfare.

The socialist believes in power and class conflict, not individualism and freedom. If there were a socialist Bible, it would no doubt begin with the phrase, "In the beginning, the government..."

PROFIT: GOD'S WAY OF SPREADING THE WEALTH AROUND

Earth—God's magnificent creation—is abundant. God made a wonderful home for us filled with natural bounty. And he gave people the capacity to create even more abundance by being productive and generating wealth.

Yet socialism relies on spreading the perception of scarcity. Even in America, the richest country on the planet, blessed with so many natural and human resources, there's always supposedly some devastating scarcity—money, healthcare, water, you name it—that requires a major redistribution scheme to rectify.

Imagine there are exactly 300 million potatoes in America, and we have to feed everyone out of the 300 million. If someone, such as the founder of Starbucks, has too many potatoes, then, to the socialist, that means someone else won't get any potatoes at all. Because of this fear-induced blind spot, the only option in socialism is to grab someone else's extra potato, chop it up, and hand it to the potato-less individuals. It never occurs to them to plant and harvest bigger crops of potatoes. It's simply *unfair* that some have planned, planted, nurtured, and produced excessive potatoes.

The socialist views the distribution of society's resources as a harsh, zero-sum game: there is a fixed amount of resources, so every transaction has a winner who gets something and a loser who gives it up. In other words, the success of one citizen diminishes the success of another. But can you imagine our all-loving, all-wise Heavenly Father designing the world so that one person's gain equates to another person's loss? Did God really create us to profit at the expense of one another? Can it really be true that wealth can't be expanded, but only "spread around"? Both the word of the Bible and the historical record of capitalism testify otherwise.

Why is the socialist hell-bent on taking from the successful? Contrary to the socialist view, God wants us to create wealth, which happens by adding value to other people's lives. That's not without limits, of course—He expects us to earn our living honestly. God also warns that worldly possessions present major temptations to conceit, pride, greed, and a lust for power.

Socialists often cite these warnings to argue that God disapproves of the wealthy. In particular, they cite Matthew 19:21–22, where Jesus says, "If you want to be perfect, go, sell what you have and give to the poor, and you will have treasure in heaven; and come, follow Me." But Jesus' intent here is best understood in connection with Matthew 10:37, when Jesus says, "Anyone who loves his father or mother more than me is not worthy of me; anyone who loves his son or daughter more than me is not worthy of me; and anyone who does not take his cross and follow me is not worthy of me."

This passage is no more about promoting dysfunctional families than the previous passage is about promoting socialism. The key to understanding these passages is that Jesus utilizes one central theme—nothing, absolutely nothing, must come between Him and His followers. In the first passage, it's one's possessions; in the second, it's one's immediate family. Both stories exemplify Christ's demands for complete devotion. Wealth, family, and many other things are valuable, but should not stand between you and Him. The moral of the story is sacrifice, not socialism.

In *An Introduction to the Devout Life*, St. Francis de Sales (1577–1622) explains that living a spiritually fulfilling life requires you to "make your property profitable and fruitful." He continues, "You can possess riches without being poisoned by them if you merely keep them in your home and purse, and not in your heart. To be rich in effect and poor in affection is a great happiness." He concludes, "Let us exercise this gracious gift of

EIGHT PROVEN WAYS TO RAISE A SOCIALIST

1. Withhold discipline, no matter the cost. Aside from being passé, spanking may cause nightmares about evil capitalists. Using "timeouts" may cause emotional isolation. And "withholding privileges" may hurt a teenager's self-esteem.

2. Spoil your child whenever possible. Shower him with what is fashionable and trendy. Give him whatever he wants even if he hasn't earned it. Reward his tantrums with gifts.

3. Share everything from iPods to underwear; to do otherwise would be selfish. Eliminate the use of possessives like "mine," "his," "hers," "ours," and "theirs." Remind them that you're the real owner of their toys.

4. Encourage, model and reward good excuse-creation and delivery; offer a bigger prize if a child's excuse evokes emotion. Make sure he understands that America is inherently unjust and that the deck is stacked against him.

5. Find a progressive school for your child that doesn't keep track of grades. Objective scoring systems are harsh, judgmental, biased, and promote competition.

6. Only pay your child an allowance until he gets an after-school or summer job. If responsibility and self-reliance are rewarded too early, your child may show signs of independence.

7. Emphasize feelings over reason, especially during the teen years. Avoid judgmental words like "right," "wrong", and "no." Begin as many sentences as possible with the phrase, "I feel…"

8. Meditate together upon Mother Earth with your child before bedtime and reassure him that he's special and secure within his assigned demographic subgroup.

preserving and even of increasing our temporal goods whenever just occasions present themselves."[10]

Undoubtedly, some capitalists are selfish and materialistic, but that is neither the cause nor the necessary effect of capitalism. The free market only promotes these character flaws in the same sense that driving "promotes" car accidents, eating promotes obesity, and marriage promotes divorce. Capitalism simply offers the freedom to focus on whatever you want—God, material wealth, or both. Socialism, on the other hand, focuses *exclusively* on material wealth. So who exactly is greedier? Is it the businesswoman who provides excellent service and, in exchange, receives an excellent profit? Or is it the mediocre office worker who lusts for an unearned share of that businesswoman's money? Or is it, perhaps, the politician who amasses ever greater job security with each redistribution scheme?

The Founders wanted to create winners. Inspired by the scriptures, they wanted to multiply success, not divide it into chunks of mediocrity. They knew the Creator's possibilities are not in short supply. There is infinite wealth because God is the never-ending source. When we add value to the resources we now have, we bring about opportunities for creating even more value in the future. In other words, profit is the divinely inspired dynamic that expands society's overall wealth.

For the socialist, "profit" is a filthy little word, a virtual synonym for "greed" or "self-indulgence" or "exploitation." But far from being evil, profit, in fact, is an invention of God, the special reward reserved for the risk-takers and status-quo breakers. It is the utilization of surplus resources to create even more resources. The prospect of profit inspires entrepreneurs to risk and innovate. Profits multiply wealth for the good of all. God uses our success to help others while we help ourselves. Our success blesses others. We don't succeed at the expense of others, but in service to others. This certainly seems to be the view of the Bible's many wealthy heroes, including Moses, Abraham, and Boaz.

Authentic success spills over to benefit many more people beyond the minority who accepted the risk. Becoming financially successful is not just tolerable; it is one of the most unselfish aims anyone could undertake. It is God's way of sharing abundance. No redistribution is required.

The bottom line is this: God doesn't care whether we have ten dollars or ten million. He cares where our heart is. He cares what we are living for, what we are devoted to, and what we are depending on. There is no amount of academic distinction that is sinful. Likewise, there is no amount of financial wealth that is immoral. However, either of these worldly accomplishments may swell our opinion of ourselves to the point where we stop looking to God and seek our own reflection instead. That's what we must resist—not wealth. It's not *what we have* that separates us from God; rather it's *what has us* that really matters.

PRIVATE PROPERTY:
STARVATION IS NOT A VIRTUE

Like wealth, private property is another biblically sanctioned concept that socialists reject. One of the earliest recorded real estate transactions was conducted by Abraham, who paid four hundred shekels of silver to secure a proper burial spot for his wife, Sarah. He purchased a deed of possession to Ephron's property east of Hebron, which included the field with all its trees, as well as the cave of Machpelah.[11] Noticeably, Abraham insisted on paying for this property, refusing Ephron's offer of the land as a gift.

The Founders drew a direct connection between private property, liberty, and the mandates of the Bible. As John Adams wrote, "The moment the idea is admitted into society that property is not as sacred as the laws of God, and that there is not a force of law and public justice to protect it, anarchy and tyranny commence. Property must be secured or liberty cannot exist."

This was a lesson learned in the first moments of American history. The Jamestown colony, established in 1607, initially rejected private property, instead adopting a communal system similar to socialism. Everyone worked the land together and divided up the harvest. As a result, according to colony secretary Ralph Hamor, most of the work was done by one-fifth of the men, the other four-fifths living as freeloaders.[12] Despite fertile soil and abundant game, most of the colonists died of starvation. Chaos emerged with reports of settlers eating cats, dogs, rats, and even their deceased neighbors. Then the colony converted to private property and it quickly thrived, attracting new settlers from all over Europe.[13] Hamor noted that after the switch there was "plenty of food, which every man by his own industry may easily and doth procure."[14]

A near-identical situation emerged at the Plymouth colony, which also began with a communal farming system. The governor of the colony, William Bradford, recounted that "young men that are most able and fit for labor and service" protested having to "spend their time and strength to work for other men's wives and children."[15] To correct the terrible situation, Bradford assigned each family their own parcel of land and told them to provide for themselves. And that's exactly what they did. Bradford saw a divine hand in the adoption of private property, relating that "instead of famine, now God gave them plenty." In 1624, there were even enough surpluses to begin exporting corn.[16] Bradford concluded, "The failure of this experiment of communal service, which was tried for several years, and by good and honest men proves the emptiness of the theory of Plato and other ancients, applauded by some of later times, that the taking away of private property, and the possession of it in community, by a commonwealth, would make a state happy and flourishing; as if it were wiser than God."[17]

Despite these practical lessons as well as biblical teachings, socialism seeks to minimize private property or abolish it altogether.

That's because private property spawns competition and inequality, and acts as a check on government control. And keep in mind, private property refers to more than just land. It's your home, your car, your cash, and all your other physical possessions. Socialists are free to share their own possessions with whomever they please, of course, but that's not enough for them. It's *our* possessions that capture their interest.

STEWARDSHIP AND
THE PARABLE OF THE TALENTS

If private ownership, profit, and wealth were sinful and oppressive to the poor, scripture would condemn such practice. It does not. The Bible never condemns wealth. To the contrary, scripture speaks of prosperity as a blessing. Throughout the Bible, God rewards people who please him with wealth and property. For example, when God told Solomon to ask for whatever he wanted, Solomon asked for wisdom. God was so pleased with this unselfish answer that he rewarded him not only with unmatched wisdom, but with vast riches and honor as well.[18]

Or consider the story of Job, a wealthy man who lost everything when he was tested by God.[19] Because he remained faithful to God through unimaginable adversity, God blessed and rewarded Job in the latter part of his life even more than in the first. He had the three most beautiful daughters in all the land, 14,000 sheep, 6,000 camels, 1,000 yoke of oxen, and 1,000 donkeys.[20] Today Job would be the scorn of socialists. Not only did he have more than he needed, he passed his wealth on to his children.

God ordains wealth because it provides the opportunity for individual stewardship. And God loves stewardship. Throughout the Bible, we are called to be wise and faithful stewards. Stewardship is the practice of taking care of the blessings that are entrusted to us. Stewardship can refer to taking care of money, physical talent, creative talent, relationships, children, property or physical possessions, and much more. We should also, of course, be good stewards of our nation. Stewardship is a great concept to teach our kids because it is all about taking care of things, and that capability might just come in handy when they start caring for us one day.

But stewardship requires ownership. Ownership can be mental, meaning that one takes responsibility for his own work and the choices he has made. Or it can be physical or financial, such as ownership of our home or savings account. True stewardship, though, flows from earned ownership. When we own something as the result of our labor, it pleases God. And the socialist is meddling in God's business when he tries to dodge natural law. When everyone is simply given things, as in the socialist model, no one really owns anything. There is no appreciation, no accountability, and consequently, no stewardship.

One of the greatest illustrations of God's expectation of stewardship is told in the Parable of the Talents, beginning in Matthew 25:14. Parables illustrate spiritual principles that apply beyond obvious spiritual matters. God uses all of scripture and especially the parables to teach us spiritual lessons and lessons about life in general. In fact, it's more accurate to say that spiritual lessons are life lessons. It is we, not God, who have insisted on separating life into the spiritual and the secular. To God, it's all spiritual. We came from someplace and we are going someplace, and what we do in between matters greatly.

In the Parable of the Talents, Jesus relates the story of a master who gives three of his servants money—he gives five talents to one servant, two to another, and one to the third. The first two servants invest their talents and double their money, and this pleases their master. Having simply buried his talent in the ground, the third servant earns his master's fury.

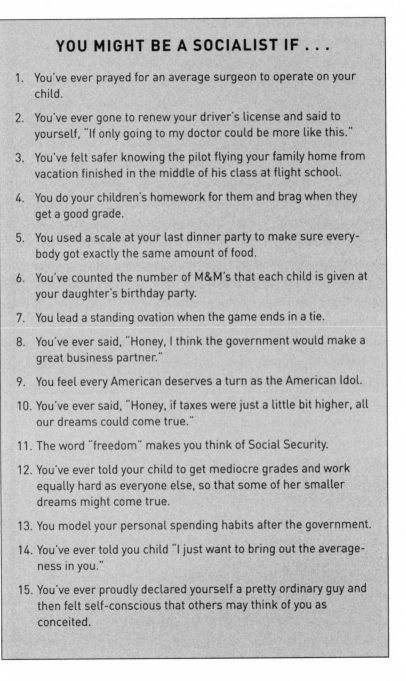

YOU MIGHT BE A SOCIALIST IF . . .

1. You've ever prayed for an average surgeon to operate on your child.

2. You've ever gone to renew your driver's license and said to yourself, "If only going to my doctor could be more like this."

3. You've felt safer knowing the pilot flying your family home from vacation finished in the middle of his class at flight school.

4. You do your children's homework for them and brag when they get a good grade.

5. You used a scale at your last dinner party to make sure everybody got exactly the same amount of food.

6. You've counted the number of M&M's that each child is given at your daughter's birthday party.

7. You lead a standing ovation when the game ends in a tie.

8. You've ever said, "Honey, I think the government would make a great business partner."

9. You feel every American deserves a turn as the American Idol.

10. You've ever said, "Honey, if taxes were just a little bit higher, all our dreams could come true."

11. The word "freedom" makes you think of Social Security.

12. You've ever told your child to get mediocre grades and work equally hard as everyone else, so that some of her smaller dreams might come true.

13. You model your personal spending habits after the government.

14. You've ever told you child "I just want to bring out the average-ness in you."

15. You've ever proudly declared yourself a pretty ordinary guy and then felt self-conscious that others may think of you as conceited.

It's hard to imagine a clearer repudiation of socialist principles. First, the parable rejects equality for merit: the master gave his servants different amounts of money, according to what each could handle effectively. Second, it endorses stewardship: the master was pleased with the first two servants because they were both good stewards of what they were given.

Perhaps most important, the story rejects the victim mentality and excuse-making. This was the approach of the third servant, who suggested his master was unfair, greedy, and possibly corrupt, then blamed his decision to bury his talent on his overwhelming fear of his master. Unlike so many leaders today, however, the master was not cowed by this counterfeit appeal to compassion. Instead, he gave the servant's single talent to the servant who'd earned ten—that is, to the most successful servant—and then ordered the "worthless slave" into the outer darkness where there would be weeping and gnashing of teeth. He summed up his attitude by saying that if you demonstrate good stewardship, you will experience abundance, and if you aren't faithful with what you have, no matter how little it is, you will lose even that.

The old Boy Scout rule is to leave things in as good a condition as you found them. But the Parable of the Talent goes beyond that, insisting we should make things *better* than we got them. It seems God is not so interested in how much we have; he wants to see what we do with whatever we've got, whether we multiply it or diminish it. In light of that, consider this question: what are the chances that the creator and owner of the largest assortment of real estate in the universe would be a socialist?

THE JOB CREATOR AND
THE VINEYARD WORKERS

In another parable, the Parable of the Vineyard Workers, Jesus tells the story of a wealthy landowner who goes out early in the morning to hire laborers for his vineyard. After agreeing on compensation of a denarius for the day, the laborers begin working. A few hours later, the landowner hires some more laborers, and this is repeated three more times throughout the day, with the last set of workers arriving at the eleventh hour.

At the end of the day, the landowner pays all the workers the same amount, regardless of when they arrived. As you might imagine, this upsets the earliest arriving workers who labored the longest. But when they complain about the unfair arrangement, the landowner curtly reminds them that he'd kept his promise to pay them a denarius, and he insists he can pay the others however much he wants.

Aside from the spiritual lessons, this story is rich in life wisdom and offers some lessons relevant to our discussion here. First, this wealthy man, the master, clearly owns and has possession of his own property. Second, as is almost always the case, the wealthy are job creators, providing work and income to men who would otherwise remain idle. Third, the laborers are paid after they do their work, not before. Success is not like a fancy restaurant where you get to eat before you pay. In the real world, you work and then you eat. Fourth, the parable illustrates the *subjective* value of work—the business owner has the leeway to pay his workers whatever he wants, not what someone else deems to be "fair." Finally, in the disgruntled workers, we see envy rearing its ugly head, as they begrudge those who secured a better deal for themselves.

Once again, scripture leaves socialism out in the cold.

GOD LOVES EXCELLENCE

Just observe His creation and you'll see that God loves excellence. The human heart beats 40 million times a year with no days off; and although the human brain weighs only three or four pounds, it contains about 100 billion neurons, which happens to be about the same number of stars as inhabit our galaxy. God made each individual person with the utmost precision. Just look at our DNA. If transcribed into English, the DNA in a single human cell would fill a 1,000-volume set of encyclopedias approximately 600 pages each.[21] The average adult carries with him about 100 trillion cells in various sizes and shapes, and with different functions and life expectancies.[22] And consider that the moon is positioned just the right distance from earth to control the tides and prevent us from needing a really big boat!

God made the world excellent, and he intended us for excellence as well. From Proverbs through the parables, God loves excellence, prudence, and productivity. Here's a sampling:

1. "In all labor there is profit, but idle chatter leads only to poverty."[23]
2. "Whatever your hand finds to do, do it with all your might."[24]
3. "When you eat or drink or do anything else, always do it to honor God."[25]
4. "Commit to the LORD whatever you do, and your plans will succeed."[26]
5. "Let the thief steal no more, but rather let him be industrious, making an honest living with his own hands, so that he may be able to give to those in need."[27]
6. "A lazy man buries his hand in the bowl, and will not so much as bring it to his mouth again."[28]
7. "Do you see a man who excels in his work? He will stand before kings."[29]
8. "The plans of the diligent lead surely to plenty."[30]
9. "Do not love sleep, lest you come to poverty."[31]

10. "The desire of the lazy man kills him, for his hands refuse to labor."[32]

In scripture, excellence is honored and indolence is condemned. Painful as it may be for some of our present leaders to digest, this is the stubborn truth. And it's really just common sense. In his second letter to the Thessalonians, the apostle Paul emphasized several fundamentals of successful living. When it came to the work ethic, he wrote,

> You surely know that you should follow our example. We didn't waste our time loafing, and we didn't accept food from anyone without paying for it. We didn't want to be a burden to any of you, so night and day we worked as hard as we could. We had the right not to work, but we wanted to set an example for you. We also gave you the rule that if you don't work, you don't eat.
>
> Now we learn that some of you just loaf around and won't do any work, except the work of a busybody. So, for the sake of our Lord Jesus Christ, we ask and beg these people to settle down and start working for a living. Dear friends, you must never become tired of doing right. Be on your guard against any followers who refuse to obey what we have written in this letter. Put them to shame by not having anything to do with them.[33]

This couldn't be more contrary to socialism, which inhibits excellence by rewarding mediocrity, pardoning irresponsibility, and artificially leveling results and rewards without corresponding merit. Hard work, long hours, and quality output are not simply unrewarded, they are often penalized.

The socialist also believes time and effort trump results. To him, just like everything else, all work should be equal. This means effort is valued as much as or more than results, and people should be compensated for effort regardless of the quality or timeliness of the work done. To a socialist, if you work for an hour and produce nothing, you should still be compensated just for showing up. As Karl Marx wrote, "We should not say that one man's hour is worth another man's hour, but rather that one man during an hour is worth just as much as another man during an hour. Time is everything, man is nothing: he is at the most time's carcass."[34]

So it doesn't matter whether you drive a truck, sell million dollar accounts, dig ditches, extract brain tumors, manage ten people, or run a billion dollar conglomerate—all work has equal inherent value. You put in an hour's work, you should get paid according to your effort or time and possibly according to your need, but *not* according to the result you produce or the value you create.

Follow the "logic" here? If society rewards better results, some people might produce better results, and that would ultimately lead to inequality of income, and that's not fair. Socialists just can't abide that kind of freedom, where individuals can rise to the height of their dreams, goals, and work ethic.

SOCIALISM: IT *SOUNDS* REALLY NICE

Sounding best to those who understand it the least, socialism is a road paved with good intentions. It highlights some legitimate grievances, and sometimes draws attention to real injustices. But as any smart preacher, counselor, or detective could verify, the best of lies are peppered ever so effectively with bits of truth. Socialism limits freedom, depresses excellence, and rewards mediocrity. Socialist practices put arbitrary and artificial limits on personal ambition, suffocating the divine spark of innovation that has historically increased prosperity for millions—and will continue to do so, if it's not snuffed out in the near or distant future.

Professing values that contradict the fundamental principles of the Bible, socialism is not the way, the truth, or the light. And can we really expect the continued blessings of God if we continue ignoring the laws of God? As Thomas Jefferson wrote, "God who gave us life gave us liberty. Can the liberties of a nation be secure when we have removed a conviction that these liberties are the gift of God? Indeed I tremble for my country when I reflect that God is just, that His justice cannot sleep forever."[35]

The free market is not perfect, but that's no reason to accept the terrible injustices of socialism. Recall Henry van Dyke's remark, "The best rose bush, after all, is not that which has the fewest thorns, but that which bears the finest roses."[36] Capitalism is in alignment with natural law and in harmony with man's instincts. It's also simple to explain, and remember, simplicity is one of God's most valuable trademarks. Socialism, to the contrary, is convoluted, violates natural law, and opposes man's positive natural instincts.

One of the main reasons our nation has been richly blessed is that our system of liberties, rooted in free will, has allowed individuals to flourish, to come alive as artists and athletes, as entrepreneurs and entertainers, as school teachers and firefighters, as corporate tycoons and political leaders. This is a good thing. God made us not as a group, but as purpose-filled, individual souls.

Finally, ancient scripture spells out indirectly, but nevertheless quite clearly, the natural instinct of healthy "self-interest" in the second most important instruction of all time: "Love your neighbor *as yourself.*"[37] The barometer for how we are to care for others is nothing less than the assumed high standard for how much we esteem ourselves. If we were expected to despise ourselves or treat ourselves shabbily, this teaching would make no sense.

This command is not about being smug or arrogant. Rather it reveals that we, by design, value ourselves highly and look out for our own interests. Even for stubborn folks like me, the moral should sink in: treat other people as well as you treat yourself, if not better. This philosophy, not greed and gluttony, guides capitalism. History shows that free markets are conducive to individual freedom, prosperity, and faith, while socialism results in stultified, atheistic nihilism.

In the end, socialism and scripture are incompatible. The Bible elevates our best instincts—kindness, self-sufficiency, generosity, and love—while socialism encourages envy, dependence, and hatred. Socialism also over-emphasizes emotion, but there is no instruction in all of scripture to make decisions based on what feels right at the moment; rather, we're taught to act according to biblical principle whether or not we happen to feel like it.

There is an old parable that speaks of a wise man and a foolish man. I presume both had good intentions. The wise man, though, built his house on a rock. And when the storms came, it stood strong. Then there was the foolish man who built his home on sand. When the rain came down and the winds blew and the streams rose, his house fell with a great crash.[38]

In practice, socialism is like building on the sand. We must not be misled; socialism will not spread success, it will spread mediocrity. And should we not correct course soon, we must expect nothing less than the great crash of our American experiment. We cannot let this happen.

We must not believe in this kind of change.

CHAPTER EIGHT

RECLAIMING CHARACTER, RESTORING VIRTUE

"Today it would be progress if everyone would stop talking about values. Instead, let us talk, as the Founders did, about virtues."

—GEORGE WILL

IN AMERICA, WE ARE ALL RICH WITH CHOICE. And our choices reveal who we really are. We have unprecedented freedom to make ourselves and our lives into something that excites and pleases us. As Americans, we can earn *inequality* with fellow citizens by developing our character. And that's what determines success in America—not birth status, or ethnicity, or even natural ability, but character.

Despite all the opportunities for people of character, however, we are living in a time marked by a surplus of information and a deficit of wisdom. Consequently many essential virtues, on both the personal and national levels, from generations past have been packed away and abandoned. This began long before the advent of the Obama administration, whose existence is both a symptom and a cause of this drift.

America launched into greatness because we had great leaders who took responsibility, exercised courage, and persisted until they got what they wanted. These rugged individualists like Thomas Paine, Patrick Henry, George Washington, Thomas

Jefferson, John Adams, Ben Franklin, and Samuel Adams had the right stuff. America continued to prosper because virtue was expected, encouraged, and rewarded.

Of course, adhering to these virtues will produce great results anywhere. But so far, freedom in America has allowed the greatest opportunity for the greatest number of people in history to attain their dreams. This is what we're fighting for—the perpetuation of the American Dream.

This chapter presents a short course in getting what you want in life—in living the Dream. The great news is that the virtues presented here can all be learned and developed. And if we Americans can relearn them, we'll open the door to our nation's renewal.

If we are to rejuvenate this great land, it will be virtues and character, not government programs, that make it happen. We must return to the sound fundamentals of success both as individuals and as a nation. And should we succeed in defeating the War on Success, it'll be a heck of a comeback indeed, and one to celebrate for many generations to come.

CHARACTER BRINGS LASTING SUCCESS

The hallmark of a highly successful person is her character. She is fiercely responsible, owning her choices and accepting the consequences of her actions no matter the personal cost. She is completely honest with herself and others in all situations. She has high standards and expects the best from herself and everyone around her. She faces her fears, thinks independently, and lives outside her comfort zone.

She is clear about what's important and what's not. She knows what she wants, why she wants it, and the road that will take her there. She demonstrates self-mastery by thinking long term, delaying gratification, and doing what must be done when it needs to be done. She outworks her competition and makes a habit of putting into something far more than she expects to take out. She insists on earning her rewards in life and refuses to seek or accept something for nothing.

As the nineteenth century success pioneer Orison Swett Marden wrote,

> The sculptor will chip off all unnecessary material to set free the angel. Nature will chip and pound us remorsefully to bring out our possibilities. She will strip us of wealth, humble our pride, humiliate our ambition, let us down from the ladder of fame, will discipline us in a thousand ways, if she can develop a little character. Everything must give way to that. Wealth is nothing. Position is nothing. Fame is nothing. Character is everything.

Our character is the essence of who we are. It's the sum total of our thoughts and habits, our vices and virtues. Character isn't part of our DNA. Rather, it's something that develops throughout our life with each and every choice we make. Ralph Waldo Emerson wrote, "Character is higher than intellect."[1] And Helen Keller, who knew something about character, said, "Character cannot be developed in ease and quiet. Only through experience of trial and suffering can the soul be strengthened, vision cleared, ambitions inspired and success achieved."

Trying to avoid adversity is like trying to avoid life. If we're somehow able to hide from adversity, we're unlikely to really be living. If we never had tough times, we would never really appreciate the great times. What would triumph mean to us if it were not partnered with strain and struggle?

To be sure, we never quite know what someone is made of until they are squeezed, until they are put under fire. Just as a pressed orange never yields apple juice, nothing comes out of people unless it's already inside them, a part of who they are.

We often expend so much energy trying to avoid adversity that when it finally comes, we're too exhausted to deal with it creatively. But adversity develops our character just as weight training develops our muscles. Like weight training, adversity is not particularly enjoyable when we're in the middle of it, but it can produce great results. Weight training speeds up our metabolism and makes us look and feel better. It makes us stronger and more resilient to accidents and all sorts of trauma. Our physical muscles become stronger when confronted with resistance, and the same is true for the muscles in our mind, spirit, and character.

Character is built by adversity, but it's neither the exclusive result of adversity nor of success. Rather, it's the effect of how we choose to respond to the circumstances of life. Both success and setbacks can shape us into something exceptional or something entirely unremarkable. It's how we respond to the adversity or success and what we learn from it that upgrades our character. James Allen explains, "The outer world of circumstance shapes itself to the inner world of thought, and both pleasant and unpleasant external conditions are factors which make for the ultimate good of the individual. As the reaper of his own harvest, man learns both by suffering and bliss."[2]

It's essential that we understand the character of success. Developing character has a lot to do with managing and mitigating the downside of human nature. Character flaws are like cracks in the foundation of an otherwise solid structure. As compromises multiply, standards shrink.

We used to be a nation of character; now many of our formative ideals are popularly disparaged. If, in 2010, we possess unshakable character rooted in Judeo-Christian beliefs, we're likely to be ridiculed as narrow-minded and judgmental—and these are just the printable epithets.

If we want to bring real change to the nation, we have to start on the inside. This doesn't mean inside the beltway. It means we have to start equipping our children with the creative thinking and good ideas that will free them to maximize their potential and become productive members of society. Everyone can play a role in helping America re-establish its foundation and reach new heights. We shouldn't leave anyone behind, child or adult. But we must lead them forward, not carry them.

SUCCESS FLOWS FROM CHARACTER

For America to develop its full potential, its leaders must emulate and encourage the character development and individual success of its citizens.

Right now, however, the President of The United States, assisted by his political and media allies, bombards Americans with the erroneous and disempowering message that success only happens to the privileged or fortunate few. Being successful is equated to winning the lottery or scoring big at the crap shoot of life.

These disingenuous words (which actually come from the president's teleprompter) portray the working rich as unworthy of the very success they've earned. Why would we want to tear down those who have lived their dream? Why wouldn't we want to interview them and study them and figure out how they reached such lofty goals? Wouldn't it be wiser to emulate them than to malign and marginalize them? In one of his lectures, the president lumped successful people in the same category as Bernie Madoff. That would be like me lumping together all Illinois politicians with the state's indicted former governor, Rod Blagojevich.

The president also routinely implies that the successful have typically achieved their success dishonestly. This is an interesting argument from Obama considering his deep ties to Tony Rezko, an Illinois real estate developer who was convicted on fraud, corruption, and money laundering charges. What's more, Obama's claim is overtly deceptive. Eighty percent of millionaires in America are self-made.[3] Even way back in 1892, 84 percent of millionaires were classified as "nouveau riche, having reached the top without the benefit of inherited wealth."[4] And when it comes to billionaires, 68 percent are self-made, with an average net worth of $4 billion.[5] This "self-made" element has long been a distinctive feature of the American experiment in which we should all take pride.

Success is democratic. Convincing research now refutes the notion that success stems from inborn gifts and talents. As *Fortune* magazine noted, "The first major conclusion is that nobody is great without work. It's nice to believe that if you find the field where you're naturally gifted, you'll be great from day one, but it doesn't happen. Across a wide range of fields, there is no evidence of high-level performance without experience or practice."[6] According to researchers, the best in any field consistently work harder and practice longer than most everyone else. *Fortune* explains,

> The critical reality is that we are not hostage to some naturally granted level of talent. We can make ourselves what we will. Strangely, the idea is not popular. People hate abandoning the notion that they would coast to fame and riches if they found their talent. But that view is tragically constraining, because when they hit life's inevitable bumps in the road, they conclude that they just aren't gifted and give up.... The liberating news is that greatness isn't reserved for a preordained few. It's available to you and to everyone.[7]

This reminds me of a joke I tell my clients: "There are lots of Michael Jordans driving beer trucks."

Here's a good way to think about success: imagine trying to hit a dart board in a room with no lights on. Even in the dark you would eventually hit the board, and if you continued long enough you may even hit a bull's eye. But if you turned on the lights, studied the techniques of excellent dart throwers, and invested ample time to practice, you would dramatically improve your performance.

When you finally hit the bull's eye, many people would call you "lucky" or "privileged." But you weren't lucky, and other than being an American, you weren't privileged either. You were just willing to pay the price and do more things to enable you to hit your target. Attributing success to luck only serves to promote government and those in power as the solution for all our problems, thus creating a debilitating mindset of dependence.

Demonizing the successful sounds more like a European perspective than an American one, doesn't it? We can view those who are more successful as role models or we can resent them. We can learn from them or be jealous of them. We can get better or we can become bitter. We can waste valuable energy whining about what others have, or we can invest our talents and energy earning what we want.

Fortunately, most of us still grasp the truth that success is within our control and that we are in charge of our destiny. In a Pew Research Center poll, 67 percent of Americans rejected the notion that success is determined by forces outside their control.[8] And according to Rasmussen Reports, 70 percent of likely voters now favor a government that offers fewer services and imposes lower taxes over one that provides more services with higher taxes.[9]

The American people clearly believe in individual success. The current government, however, is furiously trying to eradicate it.

THE MIRACLE OF CASCADING SUCCESS

Let's look at success in a bit more detail. Specifically, let's describe the prosperity cascade created by a single entrepreneur with just one employee. To begin with, that entrepreneur has created a job—two, if you include her own. Her employee uses her salary to put a down payment on her first home. As a result, two real estate agents earn a commission. That enables one of the agents to pay off her credit card debt, allowing her to live responsibly and enjoy peace of mind. The other agent is able to take a long-awaited vacation to Hawaii with her husband.

As a result of this trip to Hawaii, the airline generates revenue, along with the Hawaiian hotels, restaurants, attractions, and rental car companies. Additionally, a teenager earns a little spending money house-sitting while the couple is traveling. With the extra spending cash, the teenager takes his girlfriend out for a nice dinner, making money for the restaurant owner and earning a tip for the server. With the additional profit from this and other customers, the restaurant owner can hire a manager so that he can have more time with his family and to concentrate on growing the business. With his tip, the server can pay for gas on the way home and buy some flowers for his wife. The wife benefits, the owner of the gas station benefits, the oil company benefits, the local and state governments that collect tax benefit, and so on.

Now multiply this by 100, by 1,000, by 100,000. Consider Hobby Lobby's founder and CEO David Green, who is responsible for 16,000 jobs.[10] Or, how about Bernie Marcus and Arthur Blank, who together via Home Depot have created more than 300,000 jobs.[11] The value created in the marketplace by the individuals who take the initiative, risk their own futures, and pour their hearts into serving others in the free marketplace should be celebrated, not demonized.

Now ask yourself some questions: Why would a politician portray business owners as evil, selfish, unpatriotic, and the cause of other people's problems? What would happen if these entrepreneurs stopped working, or if they all just took a month off? Where would the economy be without these individual producers?

As Calvin Coolidge said, "No enterprise can exist for itself alone. It ministers to some great need, it performs some great service, not for itself, but for others; or failing therein, it ceases to be profitable and ceases to exist." And Napoleon Hill wrote, "No man can rise to fame and fortune without carrying others along with him. It simply cannot be done."[12]

Success is a multiplier, not a divider as this administration often suggests. Success is our Creator's way of multiplying abundance. And there's a lot more hope in that truth than in class warfare. Besides, success is not just about what we have, it's about what we do with what we have, and who we become as a result of the effort. Success, as Booker T. Washington said, is to be measured not so much by the position that one has reached in life as by the obstacles which he has overcome.

One simply has to take a quick glimpse around the globe to see the destructive consequences that eventually catch up to those countries that penalize their achievers; those countries which, in the name of "equality and compassion," bring down their successful few only to realize too late that they are demolishing the foundation of their entire nation.

FIGHTING MEDIOCRITY

If we continue to allow our leaders to butcher success while we conform to the notion that everything is relative, then can we really blame anyone but ourselves for the crooked path on which we're traveling? The late writer Irving Kristol raised a valid point: "It's hard to rise above poverty if society keeps deriding the human qualities that allow you to escape from it."[13] Or as Mark Twain put it, "It's not what a man knows that hurts him; it's what he knows that just ain't so that hurts him."

We now have generations of clueless Americans who don't even know what they don't know. Compounding this is a rather large pack of politicians who seem pleased with the helplessness of their constituents and the opportunities for interference that it provides. But America was founded as a place where we could determine our own destiny without government meddling. Consider Ayn Rand's observation: "An individualist is a man who says: I will not run anyone's life—nor let anyone run mine. I will not rule nor be ruled. I will not be a master nor a slave. I will not sacrifice myself to anyone— nor sacrifice anyone to myself." Can we rediscover the rugged individualist? Can we reclaim the right stuff? Can we rescue our distinct character before it's too late?

A story I heard as a boy speaks directly to our nation's condition today. It went like this: Little Scotty really wanted to play with his dad, and his dad really wanted to read his massive Sunday paper. Well, Scotty kept tapping on the newspaper, and finally his dad had an idea: he tore out a page of the paper that had a map of the world. He tore it into puzzle pieces and said, "As soon as you put this picture together, I'll play with you." Two minutes later his son

MASTERING MEDIOCRITY IN TEN SIMPLE STEPS

1. Tolerate average standards for yourself.

2. Hang out with moaners and complainers.

3. Make a habit of doing the minimum.

4. Look for the worst in people and situations.

5. Blame others for your mistakes and disappointments.

6. Harbor resentment and discontent.

7. Mock the successful around you.

8. Practice group-think about issues both large and small.

9. Waste as much time as possible.

10. Predict the worst about your future.

showed up with the picture together. Dad said, "Scotty, how did you put this picture of the whole world together so fast?" Scotty replied, "Daddy, it was easy. There was a picture of a man on the other side. If you put the man together right, the world goes together just fine."

In America today, we hear so much talk about society's problems, or the problems of some particular group, but we seldom, if ever, witness a real solution. Why do we maintain the habit of looking to the federal government to fix society? They have a terrible track record. And that's because society's problems are people problems. Society is nothing more than a group of individuals. And people problems are character problems that must be solved on the individual level. Instead of trying to rebuild healthcare or rebuild the economy, why don't we concentrate on rebuilding the character of the American citizenry?

This is the formula for real change; real change comes from within. After all, what happens in our houses is far more important than what happens in the White House. The ideas that follow are intended to be part of a permanent, character-based solution to our national condition today.

VIRTUES WORTH ESTABLISHING

James Allen wrote, "Of all the beautiful truths pertaining to the soul none is more gladdening or fruitful of divine promise and confidence than this—that man is the master of thought, the molder of character, and the maker and shaper of condition, environment, and destiny.[14] And here is a sampling of what our Founding Fathers had to say about virtue:

- "We have no government armed with the power capable of contending with human passions unbridled by morality and religion. Our constitution was made only

for moral and religious people. It is wholly inadequate
to the government of any other."
> —John Adams

- "If men of wisdom and knowledge, of moderation and
temperance, of patience, fortitude and perseverance, of
sobriety and true republican simplicity of manners, of
zeal for the honour of the Supreme Being and the welfare of the commonwealth; if men possessed of these
other excellent qualities are chosen to fill the seats of
government, we may expect that our affairs will rest on
a solid and permanent foundation."
> —Samuel Adams

- "Only a virtuous people are capable of freedom. As
nations become corrupt and vicious, they have more
need of masters."
> —Benjamin Franklin

Reflecting on these centuries-old admonitions, it seems these
men had a crystal ball, doesn't it?

These warnings all emphasize the importance of individual
virtue, and that's what we must reclaim. There are, however, many
different virtues. Which ones should we concentrate on? First, we
can strike off the list the trendy, present-day values like "tolerance," "empathy," and "diversity." These had no influence on our
Founders, and until very recently, no influence on this country
either.

Instead, let's focus on the real deal, the required elements of
character that allow us to develop our individual potential as
human beings. We develop these virtues by willfully practicing
them and by meditating upon their significance. Virtues, like muscles, must be strengthened through exercise, struggle, and resistance. We may also reinforce these virtues through study and

discussion. As always, what absorbs our attention begins to shape our thinking.

The Virtue of Courage

Courage is the character quality that allows for growth and self-mastery. It's the willingness to get outside our comfort zone and operate in the success zone. Courage is the opposite of immobilization. It's the guts and grit to do what's right *because* it's right. Both cowards and heroes face fear; their response to fear and uncertainty, however, defines who they become. Courage can be cultivated and developed through practice and repetition. As we develop more courage, we attract more opportunities. As our courage expands, so does our depth of character.

Courage is about taking the first step and also about mustering the will to press on. Courage is doing what's unpopular because it's the right thing to do. Courage is *not* doing what's popular when it's the wrong thing to do. Sticking by a friend when everyone else has abandoned her—now that's courage.

It also takes courage to stand up for our convictions when everyone else is sitting down. It takes courage to say no when everyone else is saying yes. Courage is the willingness to launch without a guarantee. It takes courage to risk failure and follow our dream. Every business in America reflects an act of courage. The great management teacher Peter Drucker said, "Whenever you see a successful business, someone once made a courageous decision." It takes courage to think independently and rise above the crowd.

American history is filled with courage, even if it's no longer recognized as much as it should be. It took courage for America's first settlers to get on those ships and sail to the unknown. It took courage for Patrick Henry to declare, "Give me liberty or give me death." It took courage for the greatest generation to storm the beaches of Normandy. It took courage for Rosa Parks to quietly refuse to give up her bus seat. It took courage for the first astronauts to launch into unchartered territory. It took courage for firefighters to rush into the World Trade Centers when everyone else was running out.

We must act courageously even when we feel uncourageous. Courage is infectious and inspiring. When others witness acts of courage, they're inspired to do likewise. Courage is the virtue that allows for the development of a rock-solid character. Courage, as Churchill observed, "is rightly considered the foremost of the virtues, for upon it, all others depend."

The Virtue of Responsibility

The mark of a fully mature, mentally healthy individual is the acceptance of complete responsibility for his life. We cannot blame others for who we are and what we become. Owning our choices is the essence of personal responsibility. The successful individual acknowledges he is the source and cause of his thoughts, feelings, actions, and results.

This doesn't mean it's our own fault whenever anything bad happens to us; it means that how we respond reveals our character. As an engineer might ask, "What happened? What do we do now?" Because we have the gift of free will, we can choose what we do with our life and how we respond to adversity.

The opposite of responsibility is blaming, whining, and excuse-making. These reactions temporarily exonerate us, much like a stiff drink, but they ultimately immobilize us and overextend our emotional line of credit. Worse yet, when we've finished blaming, we haven't improved one bit.

Many Americans have been coaxed and misled into blaming their boss, spouse, parents, kids, the weather, capitalism, and the neighbor's dog for their dissatisfactions and disappointments in life. It's a great tragedy that we have herds of discontented and underachieving people trudging around blaming everyone and everything for their lack of success. These people refuse to put the responsibility for their lives back where it belongs—with the person they see in the mirror.

Looking to oneself and inside oneself for the answer to our own problems is both scary and liberating. As the economist Thomas Sowell writes,

> Many of the issues of our times are hard to understand without understanding the vision of the world that they are part of. Whether the particular issue is education, economics or medical care, the preferred explanation tends to be an external explanation—that is, something outside the control of the individuals directly involved.... The great escape of our times is escape from personal responsibility for the consequences of one's own behavior.[15]

Escaping or evading responsibility for one's choices has virtually become a national pastime, with the government dutifully serving as the prime enabler. Somewhere along the line, responsibility was extracted from liberty. But making excuses for citizens or inventing a ridiculous concept like "mutual responsibility" does this nation and its posterity no favors. George Washington Carver said, "Ninety-nine percent of the failures come from people who have the habit of making excuses." And Ben Franklin agreed, arguing that "he that is good for making excuses is seldom good for anything else." The only thing more damaging to our character than making an excuse is making the same excuse twice.

Excuses should be laughed at, not dignified as they often are today. Excuses and responsibility cannot coexist. If there's anything in our life that's not the way we want it to be, we are responsible for changing it. Whether it's something big or small, we are still responsible, and each time we give an excuse we diminish our respect, our credibility, and our integrity in our own eyes as well as the eyes of others. Each time we make an excuse, we reinforce our propensity to make even more excuses in the future, and excuse making becomes an infectious cultural habit. As humans, we love to rationalize our ineptitude. Unless we make a commitment to the choice of excuse-free living, we'll always be able to find fresh excuses. The next time we feel the urge to utter an excuse, we should all remember the slogan of the Paralympics: *What's Your Excuse?*

Taking responsibility for our life is like being a good defensive driver. If our car is totaled in an accident, it won't provide us much comfort to know that we had a green light. The question that will resonate in our mind is, "What could we have done to prevent this?" Blaming the other driver won't help much either. It will only distract our attention from what we need to learn. We can stay empowered and in control by analyzing all unpleasant situations from the perspective of what we can do to avoid their recurrence. When we're anchored in the reality of responsibility, we're far more likely to act in ways that will not become causes of regret, frustration, or embarrassment. No one else is responsible for our own character development. "Duty," as Calvin Coolidge said, "is not collective; it is personal."

The Virtue of Integrity

Integrity is the strict adherence to our convictions. Principles matter, and integrity is honoring, or living in full alignment with, the guiding principles we have staked our life upon in all situations, no matter what. This means we don't abandon our principles when they're inconvenient, uncomfortable, unpopular, or disadvantageous in any other way. If our integrity can be bought or sold for the sake of circumstance, we are exchanging something we did not really possess in the first place.

Our integrity as individuals describes and defines what kind of person we really are at the core. And the type of person we are on the inside is reflected by the things we say and do on the outside, as well as the things we refrain from saying and doing. Consequently, people with integrity have a much easier time making decisions. Discerning right from wrong is like choosing up from down: it's clear-cut.

If we have integrity in some areas and not in others, or if we only uphold it when it's convenient, do we really have any integrity at all? Dwight Moody said, "Character is what you are in the dark." This is an obvious inspiration to live every moment like someone is watching. A life of integrity is not an easy life, but it's the simple life, and the type of life that others will seek to emulate or eventually wish they had.

Buildings with integrity are complete and structurally sound. When we have integrity, we are secure in our convictions and comfortable in our own skin. We don't have to exaggerate, distort, or misrepresent what we are all about. As one of my mentors told me, "Every addition to the truth is a subtraction from it."

Having integrity is like having plenty of money in the bank. If we don't have integrity it's like being broke. With integrity, unlike our finances, there's no middle ground. It's either something we have in full or we don't possess it at all. In any case, we can bounce back from a financial disaster, but that's not so easy to do with integrity. Individuals with high character sacrifice personal gain of any kind to preserve their integrity. Whatever the price our integrity demands, we should pay it and know that we've made a wise investment.

Those without the moral foundation of integrity often give in to the twin villains of compromise and conformity. Conceding our standards and conforming to the values of others often seems like a clever, reasonable thing to do. However, like bending the truth, compromising and conforming becomes easier with time as we progressively diminish our self-worth. Would we want our son or daughter to marry someone who compromises their integrity, even for apparently altruistic reasons?

On the political scene today, deception seems not only to be tolerated in many circles; it's applauded if "successful." When the ends justify the means, anything goes. If the ultimate objective is perceived to be virtuous, then the methods used for getting there don't matter.

With easily accessible transcripts and Internet video clips, it's easy today to spot the tools of the deceitful; word games, half-truths, and artificial complexity designed to spin, daze, and confuse an honest citizen trying to figure out what in the world is going on. An honorable leader isn't only focused on winning; he's focused on how he wins. In a commencement address, entrepreneurial legend Karl Eller summed it up:

> Without integrity, motivation is dangerous; without motivation, capacity is impotent; without capacity, understanding is limited; without understanding, knowledge is meaningless; without knowledge, experience is blind. Experience is easy to provide and quickly put to good use by people with the other qualities. Make absolute integrity the compass that guides you in everything you do. And surround yourself only with people of flawless integrity.[16]

That we live is not nearly as important as the manner in which we live. The challenge of integrity is not the challenge of perfection, but the challenge of direction. Are we leading our lives in the right direction with our daily decisions? And more important, are we living the life we were meant to live?

The Virtue of Self-Discipline

Self-discipline is the learned ability to direct our appetite and passions in a productive direction. It is the sustained capacity to do what it takes for as long as it takes. Self-discipline occurs in the moments when intention defeats indulgence, when mission trumps mood, and when spirit conquers sentiment. Self-discipline is the connective tissue that links ambition with achievement. A variable that either multiplies or divides natural talent, it's both an investment in our future and an inspiration to others. Those who are undisciplined, however, are slaves to their feelings, a condition that causes all sorts of trouble throughout one's life.

Clearly, self-discipline plays a big role in our success; fortunately, it can be cultivated through small, daily acts. Everything we value requires discipline to move it in the direction we want it to go. We become self-disciplined when we synchronize our long-term goals with our short term choices. We must first discipline our mind, keeping our thoughts on our dreams and goals and off our fears and worries. We must also exercise discipline to stay healthy and energetic. Our marriage takes discipline, as does raising responsible, self-reliant kids. And of course, our financial life is in jeopardy if we fail to discipline what we spend, save, and invest. With self-discipline, we do what we need to do, when we need to do it, whether we feel like it or not.

Look at it this way: the world can be divided into feelers and doers. Feelers take action and initiative only when they feel like doing so. We become a feeler by default, by overlooking this aspect of our character. Doers, on the other hand, act their way into feeling. We become a doer by making a deliberate decision to do so. We may conceivably be a feeler in one area and a doer in another. But without a definite decision to do otherwise and a strong dose of self-discipline, we're all prone to engage in actions

A LESSON FROM AESOP: *THE ANTS AND THE GRASSHOPPER*

One fine day in winter some Ants were busy drying their store of corn, which had got rather damp during a long spell of rain. Presently up came a Grasshopper and begged them to spare her a few grains, "For," she said, "I'm simply starving." The Ants stopped work for a moment, though this was against their principles. "May we ask," said they, "what you were doing with yourself all last summer? Why didn't you collect a store of food for the winter?" "The fact is," replied the Grasshopper, "I was so busy singing that I hadn't the time." "If you spent the summer singing," replied the Ants, "you can't do better than spend the winter dancing." And they chuckled and went on with their work.

that only produce immediate payback, and may even move us further away from where we ultimately want to be.

Today, many Americans are slaves to their feelings. If a man feels like exercising, he will. If he doesn't, he won't. If a mom feels like having that important conversation with her teenager, she will. If she doesn't, she won't. Disciplining ourselves to override unproductive emotions opens up a whole new universe of possibilities and will elevate our performance in all areas of life. As William James wrote, "Action seems to follow feeling, but really action and feeling go together; and by regulating the action, which is under the more direct control of the will, we can indirectly regulate the feeling, which is not."

I teach my clients there is a considerable difference between what we *can't* do and what we *won't* do to improve our current circumstances. *Can't* is about legitimate capability, and *won't* is about emotional willingness. Many Americans, however, blur this distinction, and that can cost them dearly.

Many people toss their bad habits in the *can't* pile when they really belong in the *won't* pile. People in financial trouble tell themselves they *can't* downgrade their lifestyle when they really mean they *won't*. Many spouses tell themselves they *can't* do what it takes to strengthen or save their marriage, when they really mean they *won't*. Many in politics tell us they *can't* stop the spending programs when they really mean they *won't*. Once we've mentally assigned a productive behavior to the *can't* pile, we tend to act helpless and, for obvious reasons, don't exert any self-discipline toward resurrecting it.

Although we live in an instant culture where *now* is no longer fast enough, self-discipline equips us to keep our impulsivity and desire for instant satisfaction in check. We sacrifice something lesser today for something greater tomorrow. High achievers are motivated by pleasurable outcomes, while underachievers are motivated by pleasurable methods. As bestselling author John Maxwell says, "Play today and pay tomorrow or pay today and play tomorrow." The philosophy reinforcing this sort of self-discipline is long-term thinking. If our time horizons are long, then we tend to make decisions that build our character and move us closer to our desired destination.

Lapses in discipline tend to multiply; fortunately, so do expressions of self-discipline. But there are no shortcuts to true success. Goethe wrote, "Knowing is not enough; we must apply. Willing is not enough; we must do." As we work to fortify the virtue of self-discipline within ourselves, we can be encouraged by the insight of business philosopher Jim Rohn, "For every disciplined effort, there is a multiple reward." Like making a deposit in our savings account, every effort of self-discipline adds up, not to our net worth but to our self-worth.

Finally, the self-disciplined individual knows that future change is an illusion. The reality is that "tomorrow" changes only as a result of what we do today. And what we do today is a measure of our self-discipline. I have found over the years that the most unhappy people in the world are those who use the word "tomorrow" most often. These individuals haven't shown up for their own life and the more they begin to realize it, the more it bothers them.

Discipline happens...eventually. Either we take the lead and discipline ourselves or nature will, at some point, step in and play the role of disciplinarian for us.

CHAPTER NINE

THE BILL OF RESPONSIBILITIES

"I recommend that the Statue of Liberty be supplemented by a Statue of Responsibility on the west coast."

—Viktor Frankl

I N ORDER TO DEFEND AND PROMOTE SUCCESS, we need to understand the principles and habits that successful people share. Exposure to these truths will change the lens through which fellow citizens view both their government and their future. It's important not only for our own success, but for our family's and our nation's success that we understand the prerequisites to reaching our full potential.

Some successful individuals follow these principles instinctively. Others have simply emulated those who organized their ambition around these ideas. Still others, hungry for success, have sought out and found these answers on their own. None of these concepts are secrets, although it often seems as if they were.

In the pages that follow, we'll discuss the principles of success, the origins of success, and the benefits of success for our society. In the process, the enemy of success will become painfully clear. Just as the opposite of love is not hate but indifference, so too, the arch enemy of success is not failure but mediocrity.

There is one theme that unites the principles presented here: independent initiative. No government program and no amount of other people's money can compensate for the lack of insight as to what it takes to get what we want in life. It's up to *you* to reach your goals. This chapter will show you how.

PRINCIPLES WORTH PRACTICING

If we're not aware of them, or worse yet, if we choose to ignore them, the principles of life tend to be equal opportunity destroyers. Take gravity. If no one ever explained the nature of gravity and we accidentally stepped off our neighbor's two-story deck, we'd all fall straight down, never up. It wouldn't make a difference if we were in a protected demographic class and had special rights; we'd still go down. That's how natural law works. It's incapable of discrimination, which is, I suppose, why social engineers harbor such antagonism toward it.

When we align our life with the timeless principles of natural law, we experience a surge of confidence, competence, and unparalleled optimism for the future. But the responsibility for learning about these principles and then living by them is completely up to each of us as individuals. We can't take the default position of simply making up our own little pet laws of life. As the old saying goes, "Ignorance of the law is no excuse." We can break man-made laws (or should that be "person-made" laws?) and frequently escape without penalty. But timeless principles have a way of tracking us down and serving us with unpleasant consequences despite our ignorance or best intentions.

If we're serious about developing all the potential within us, we must avoid the trendy *principe du jour* mentality that has smothered our society. Watch and you'll see that it's common for current political leaders to use the word "principle" in lieu of other less appealing words like "idea," "notion," "theory," "program," and "whim."

After coaching entrepreneurs for nearly twenty years, it's become clear to me that when an individual's life or business is off track, it's inevitably the result of drifting from proven principles. When entrepreneurs recalibrate with authentic principles, their business or personal life becomes more successful, productive, and harmonious. It's no mystery or accident, and the same goes for our country as a whole. Principles matter most.

What follows is not an exhaustive inventory of the principles that lead to success, but it does provide us with a running start. As you'll notice, everything flows from or relates back to the first principle mentioned earlier, the Principle of the Harvest, otherwise known as Sowing and Reaping.

The Principle of the Harvest

We all can foretell the future if we simply examine today's choices. This is because we live in an orderly universe governed by principles that work 24/7 for sinner and saint alike. As Blaise Pascal wrote, "Nature imitates itself. A grain thrown into good ground brings forth fruit; a principle thrown into a good mind brings forth fruit. Everything is created and conducted by the same Master: the root, the branch, the fruits—the principles, the consequences."[1]

Impartial and impersonal, the Harvest Principle has a clear sequence—first we sow and then we reap. This natural law was already old when the pyramids were brand new. And like gravity, it works all day, every day, everywhere in the world (except maybe D.C.), regardless of whether anyone has ever told us about it. It's simply impossible to harvest with integrity something one has not sown, though many squander their entire lives hoping and depending on this sort of arrangement with the state.

An ancient parable reminds us that we'd be wise to plant a bit more than we hope to harvest. This is because some of the seed won't bear any fruit at all. No, this is not an injustice, and it doesn't make us victims. It's just another mysterious dynamic of life. According to the story, some percentage of the seeds we sow will be taken by the birds, some will land on the rocky ground and shrivel in the heat, and some will be strangled by the weeds. Others will take root in the fertile soil and yield a lopsided crop—a hundred, sixty, or even thirty times what was sown.[2] Once we're aware of this, we can fine-tune our life strategy to be in harmony with it.

In the business world, if we want to be highly paid, we must first become valuable in the eyes of the person who signs our check. The Greek philosopher Epictetus reflected on this, saying, "Nothing great is created suddenly, anymore than a bunch of grapes or a fig. If you tell me that you desire a fig, I answer you that there must be time. Let it first blossom, then bear fruit, then ripen."[3]

Simply stated, *if we want to reap more rewards, we must sow more service, contribution, and value.* Success in life isn't based on need, but on seed. This presents us with the choice of becoming either a first-rate spring planter or a very clever fall beggar. If we want to know what we sowed in the past, we need only look around

---

THINK LIKE A WINNER!

How wealthy should we become?
As wealthy as we can.

How healthy should we become?
As healthy as we can.

How wise should we become?
As wise as we can.

How generous should we become?
As generous as we can.

How loving should we become as a spouse?
As loving as we can.

How effective should we become as a parent?
As effective as we can.

How successful should we become?
As successful as we can.

THINK LIKE A LOSER!

How wealthy should we
   become?
As wealthy as the state allows.

How healthy should we
   become?
As healthy as the state allows.

How wise should we become?
As wise as the state allows.

How generous should we
   become?
*As generous as the state
allows.*

How loving should we become
   as a spouse?
As loving as the state allows.

How effective should we
   become as a parent?
As effective as the state allows.

How successful should we
   become?
*As successful as the state
allows.*

us and see what we're reaping today. Of course, if we reap but do not sow, it means others must sow but not reap. This is a disruption of natural law, and that's never a good thing.

Unfortunately, many Americans have been deceived, confused, tricked, and even "inspired" into believing they will not be held accountable for their choices and that they'll miraculously harvest something other than what they planted. This dangerously popular distortion fuels mediocrity and underachievement. Consider the effort and expense Americans undertake to solve and cure diseases and social problems while they do very little, if anything, to avoid them. It's popular to treat the symptom of a problem, but it's often considered "insensitive," "judgmental," or "intolerant" to speak of or address the root causes of the assorted predicaments people find themselves in.

As a result, an attitude percolates throughout our nation denying that effects really have causes. But without exception, every effect has a cause or a group of causes, even if we haven't accurately identified them yet. Consequences end up being our best teachers. And actions as well as inaction have consequences.

Success is the effect generated by strategic thinking integrated with productive action. Success occurs in the lives of specific people for specific reasons. It comes from figuring out what we want to accomplish and then choosing to invest our time doing only those things that move us down the path to our destination. It's not something that randomly happens to us; success is something that we make happen. It's not complex, and there's no magic involved. Success, however we choose to define it, is predictable.

By investing the time to find out how other people became successful, we can learn, emulate, and in due season, begin achieving similar results. Both success and failure are predictable because they follow the immutable Law of Sowing and Reaping. As Henry Wadsworth Longfellow wrote, "The heights by great men reached and kept—Were not attained by sudden flight, But they, while their companions slept—Were toiling upward in the night."[4]

We begin our climb toward our full potential as human beings the moment we accept and absorb the truth that cause and consequence are inseparable. The opposite of this truth is called "accidentalism," which asserts that events have no causes. How convenient, right? The successful citizen knows reaping requires sowing, and lots of it.

The Principle of Character

Our circumstances are simply a reflection of our character, of what we are made of as individuals. The quality of our outer life of relationships, health, and happiness mirrors the quality of our inner life of thoughts, feelings, beliefs, and expectations. Accepting this truth represents the highest plane of personal responsibility. Again, James Allen nails the truth: "Men are anxious to improve their circumstances, but are unwilling to improve themselves; they therefore remain bound."[5]

Daunting as it may be, understanding this principle means real change is an inside game that must begin with the individual and no one else. To experience a better life, first become a better person. To enjoy a better marriage, first become a better spouse. To earn more money, first provide more value and contribution. To succeed more, first become more. Napoleon Hill wrote, "Every line a man writes, and every act in which he indulges, and every word he utters serves as inescapable evidence of the nature of that which is deeply imbedded in his own heart, a confession that he cannot disavow."[6] Eventually and inevitably, cause and effect will triumph. The successful citizen looks within himself as the source of his troubles.

The Principle of Accumulation

Our life is a bundle of choices that accrue into something either really special or not so special. A successful life is simply the accumulation of thousands of efforts, often unseen by others, that lead to the accomplishment of worthwhile goals. More than any other single factor, we are where we are today and who we are today because of the choices we've made up until this moment.

I have found, somewhat recently, that decision-making is a lot like getting on a water slide. We still have options right up to the point when we launch ourselves into the tube. Once we make that decision, principles take over and consequences happen automatically. There's no turning back.

Consider some of the decisions we've all made or will make pointing to the future. Each and every one of these decisions is accompanied by at least one consequence. We've decided to believe some things and disbelieve others. We've decided when to study and when to blow off the books; what to learn and what not to learn; and who to spend our time with and who to avoid. And we've decided or will decide who we'll date, who we'll marry, whether we'll have children, and what kind of parent we'll become.

We've decided to accept responsibility and decided to blame others. We've decided to persevere and decided to give up. We've decided whether or not we'll drink, smoke, or use drugs. We've decided what we will eat or not eat. We've decided either to plan out exciting goals for our life or just to wing it. We've decided to give in to fear and decided to bravely press on. We've decided to be the best and decided to act like all the rest.

Consider for a moment all the decisions you've made in just the last year. These choices are made daily, hourly, and minute-to-minute. How might your life be different today if you had made a handful of different decisions? If we make the same decisions as most people do, we will get what most people get. And here's what that means: 49 percent of marriages now end in divorce. Eighty percent of people working today want to change jobs. More than 50 percent of Americans are overweight, one out of three will get cancer, and two out of five will suffer heart disease. More than 60 percent of Americans, living in the richest, most abundant civilization in history, will retire with little or no savings, dependent on entitlements for survival.

No offense to anyone, but America doesn't need more average people; we need more exceptional ones. Remember, no one plans to become mediocre. Mediocrity is the result of no plan at all, or worse still, a government plan.

Think about this aphorism: *Sow a thought, reap an action; Sow an action, reap a habit; Sow a habit, reap a character; Sow a character, reap a destiny.* The successful citizen leverages this principle to create an unstoppable spiral of growth and satisfaction.

The True North Principle

Too many today see truth as elastic, fluid, situational, relative, and subjective. Right and wrong are defined more often in terms of what "feels" good or what "feels" right to the individual. More precisely, truth is not just in the eye of the beholder, but in the eye of the beholder at a particular moment in time. Ravi Zacharias wrote, "The hollow lives that fill countless news stories or live in anguished silence reveal the price paid for the belief that truth as a category does not exist."

The "True North" Principle, however, insists *there are still fixed truths of right and wrong,* despite the sea of moral relativity that now surrounds us. Disavowing these truths doesn't block their impact on our life. These absolute truths are rooted in the Bible and comprise the natural law from which the Framers of the Constitution established our republic. The fact that many in political power today deny these American roots doesn't change the fact that these are our heritage and form the very foundation of our freedom.

Clearly, the further we have distanced ourselves from these truths, the more morally lost we have become as a people, while our societal, cultural, and political problems have grown. To the degree that we as individuals or as a nation line up our choices to be in harmony with natural law, we experience predictable success and satisfaction. To the degree that we ignore True North we experience frustration, underachievement, and inevitable regret in the long run.

The successful know what they stand for, and conversely, what they won't fall for; they defend their convictions.

The Reality Principle

We must deal with the world the way it really is, not the way we wish it were. Uncover the facts. Study history. Seek the truth. Remain objective. As Ronald Reagan liked to say, "Facts are stubborn things." Until we can acknowledge how the world really works, and where we are in relation to where we'd rather be, we aren't free to go forward in wisdom and improve upon our current situation. This holds true for our business career, our marriage, our health, and every other aspect of our life. We must quickly discriminate between unalterable facts and solvable problems.

We have to "tell it like it is," not like we wish it were. We have to level with ourselves and demonstrate intellectual honesty. We have to acknowledge the truth, even if it's ugly, before we can improve upon it. As mentioned earlier, political correctness frequently interferes with the practice of the reality principle because it renders certain topics off limits and deters people from dealing with the truth. The right perspective can change everything. Often, we need to step back and get out of the frame before we can see the whole picture. If blunders have been made, we can ask for forgiveness, maturely accept the consequences of our mistakes, and move on.

The more brutally honest we are with ourselves, the more effective we can be in correcting course on the path to our goals. Where are you in life compared with where you want to be? Where are we as a country compared with where we could be and should be? Notice that the successful tend to avoid self-deception and deal directly with the reality of their circumstances.

The Principle of Clarity

The clearer we are about what we intend to accomplish, the more likely we will observe the means of attaining it. Likewise, the more tentative, ambiguous, and vague we are in defining what we are pursuing, the more prone we'll be to waste time, mismanage resources, and become distracted. By specifying our objectives, we heighten our awareness, minimize confusion, and eliminate hesitancy. We all need a great and distant goal toward which to strive. And precisely worded goals tell our brains what to notice, what to pay attention to, and in what direction to move. Our goals highlight our values.

When we're extremely clear about what we want, we have the power supply for our ambition. If we're unclear about our destination, it's as though we're disconnected or unplugged from that power supply and the progress that it generates. Most underperformance can be traced back to confusion about an objective. Insufficient clarity about what is truly important is the root of most interpersonal conflicts as well. The successful citizen knows what she wants, why she wants it, and how she's going to accomplish it.

The Principle of the Path

This principle, well-articulated by leadership expert Andy Stanley, states that *it is our direction, not our intention, that determines our destination*.[7] This is true for an organization, a married couple, an individual, and most especially a nation. We succeed in life (in other words, wind up in our preferred spot) to the degree that we accurately determine and then stay on the road that leads us to the achievement of our goal. We succeed when we make decisions, over and over again, that move us in the direction of our predetermined destination while veering off course as little as possible. The successful citizen always and only expects to reach her goal when she's been traveling down the right path.

The Principle of Attention

Whatever holds our attention molds our intention. Whatever we emphasize with our thoughts, words, or deeds multiplies in our mind. Naturally, whatever we ignore begins to atrophy and fade away. At any given moment, we can choose to pay attention to what's present or what's missing, what's working or what's broken, what we achieved or what we messed up, what's available or what's unavailable, what's possible or what's impossible, and what excites us or what frightens us. The longer we can sustain a positive mental image, the more progress we'll make and the more gratitude we can enjoy. No area of our life is untouched by our thoughts.

Although people aren't automatically positive, neither are we hopelessly negative. Our life tends to imitate the thoughts that we entertain most consistently. The corollary of this is that we feel what we dwell upon. To experience more joy in life, we can reflect and meditate upon our blessings. If we care to experience less joy, we can always dwell upon our disappointments and shortcomings. Successful citizens focus on blessings and opportunities.

The Principle of Belief

Our life is a derivative of our beliefs, and we can only change our beliefs by changing the thought patterns that structure the belief itself. Whatever we believe long and deeply enough usually comes to pass. A belief is simply a collection of habitual thoughts that represent what we consider to be the truth about any given situation or circumstances in our life. Our beliefs are worth understanding because we always act in a manner consistent with what we truly believe despite what we might otherwise say. It's not our words, though, but our actions that illuminate our true beliefs.

We can learn a lot about ourselves by reflecting on the things we do repeatedly. This is important because our actions, fused to our beliefs, either take us down the productive path or the unproductive path. Typically, people want to change their results, but they don't want to or know how to amend the underlying belief. This causes the "bungee" dynamic. Certain individuals strong enough to force a positive change via their own will power can experience a better result, but only temporarily, until the cord bounces back to its original length as a result of deeply entrenched beliefs. This explains a host of chronic struggles like weight loss and relationship issues.

If we desire to reach our full potential, we must sooner or later confront limiting beliefs and replace them, like a software upgrade, with effective beliefs that keep us moving toward the intended destination. The successful citizen accepts that beliefs precede circumstances.

The Principle of Expectation

In the long run, we tend to receive not what we want out of life, but what we boldly expect to receive. We know we've found the sweet spot when our wants and our expectations melt into each other. What we expect and confidently prepare for tends to materialize in our lives, and often sooner than we could have imagined. It's our optimistic preparation, though, that reveals our true expectation or lack thereof. Frequently, we desire something awesome, but get ready for something average. Too often, our best case scenario is undermined by our own thoughts, words, or behaviors. Too often, we pray for sunshine and then grab our umbrella. We should assume great news and think, speak, and act accordingly. The successful citizen engineers this principle in his favor by preparing as though the realization of his biggest goal was inevitable and unavoidable.

The 80/20 Principle

The vast majority of what we do makes very little difference, especially in the long run. Conversely, a small number of actions make a huge impact. In most businesses, 80 percent of the revenue is generated by only 20 percent of the sales force, meaning the team's success relies on a small, super-productive minority. Likewise, in life, typically 80 percent of our results will come from

20 percent of our efforts. When we start employing 80/20 think-ing in our daily lives, it can revolutionize our world.

This principle and the mindset it produces help explain why some people are exponentially more effective and successful than others. Unfortunately, only a tiny fraction of the working popu-lation applies this law of productivity in their work, and even fewer do so in their family life, despite the dramatic break-throughs other peak performers have reported. We can never do everything; therefore, we must figure out what are the most valu-able priorities and execute them consistently.

As a spouse, there are only a few things that we can do that make a really big difference in our marriage. Have we identified them? With our health and longevity, there are just a handful of things that are considered critical to our energy and wellness. Have we identified them? As a parent, there are only a few things we can do to really influence our child's most important decisions. Have we identified them? In our career, there are just a few things that will really impact our future success. Have we identified them?

This is a powerful principle that can and should be used every day—my wife even accuses me of wearing 20 percent of my shirts 80 percent of the time.

The Principle of Association

We become like the people with whom we spend most of our time. We are, in effect, human sponges soaking up the values, world-view, beliefs, habits, and even the speech patterns, body language, and mannerisms of the individuals with whom we associate. Our family, friends, and coworkers can sway us in the direction we have predetermined to travel, or they can ever so gradually nudge us down an alternate path.

Years ago, one of my coaches asked me if I understood the two reasons why I should never wrestle with a pig. I said, "No, what are they?" He replied, "First, you'll just get dirty and second, the pig will like it." This is a very uncomfortable truth. The people with whom we choose to spend our time have a disproportionate influence on our thinking and, by extension, on how productive and successful we become. A major reason people fail is because they associate with failure.

I advise my entrepreneurial clients in *The 1% Club* to spend as much time as possible with people who are similar to what they want their children to be like when they grow up. Typically, that means surrounding ourselves with ambitious, character-driven people; with individuals committed to making a positive difference in the world.

Winners tend to hang around with other winners. As Olympic champion Billy Kidd says, "If you want to be at your best, be with the best." Losers tend to hang with losers who whine and bathe in mediocrity. Birds of a feather definitely flock together. As George Washington said, "Associate with men of good quality if you esteem your own reputation; for it is better to be alone than in bad company." Other people have immense power to either distract us or inspire us. It's our responsibility to evaluate the influence that our relationships are having on our journey through life.

Good things happen when we make our most important relationships the "right relationships." Relationships have consequences. Therefore, the successful citizen looks at relationships as investments in the future.

The Principle of Resentment
We typically repel what we resent. In other words, nature works against us when we envy the lifestyle or possessions of others. It's not only wrong to break the Tenth Commandment, it's

counterproductive. Even if we're able to get something we jealously covet, we're unlikely to retain it permanently until we rightfully earn it or eliminate the resentful attitudes toward it.

The flip side of this is the good news and the real message. The fastest way to achieve what we want in life is to admire and applaud those who have already achieved it. This seems to hit a mental switch that releases all resistance to living the life of our dreams. The successful citizen talks positively about, looks up to, and appreciates the unseen efforts required to succeed at anything worthwhile and meaningful.

HABITS WORTH FOLLOWING

Habits are repetitive behaviors that have become automatic through repetition and affirmation. Every habit, whether helpful or hurtful, adds color and definition to our character. Constructive habits produce positive results and conserve willpower for other endeavors. Destructive habits become like tyrants robbing us of what might have been. Steven Covey wrote, "Our character is basically a composite of our habits. Because they are consistent, often unconscious patterns, they constantly, daily, express our character."[8] And Ben Franklin noted, "Each year one vicious habit rooted out, in time might make the worst man good throughout."

The following four habits are big-picture, strategic habits that are helpful to anyone committed to high-character, principle-driven living. Following these habits makes us stronger citizens, and stronger citizens make a better country.

The Habit of Reflection

This is the habit of deliberately glancing back and grabbing the important lesson from the past in order to make better decisions in the future. The ancient Greeks saw a lot of wisdom in this.

Socrates said, "The unexamined life is not worth living." Aristotle followed that observation with one of his own, "The unplanned life is not worth examining."

Today is the future we looked forward to ten years ago. But are we enjoying it as much as we thought we would? Are we willing to question the choices we've made? Are we willing to evaluate how well we have managed our life up until now? George Washington believed, "We ought not to look back unless it is to derive useful lessons from past errors, and for the purpose of profiting by dearly bought experience." That sums it up; reflection is looking back in order to go forward with a better perspective and more wisdom.

Due to the sheer velocity of life, though, few people regularly carve out time to critically evaluate the quality of their decisions and the direction of their life. And even fewer work out a plan for their future. Most Americans are swept along in the current of overloaded calendars and back-to-back activities for both parent and child alike. Most just act, rinse, and then repeat the same habits day after day.

As a result of this frenetic pace, dangerous blind spots develop, breakthrough opportunities are missed, irreplaceable relationships are neglected, and mistakes are repeated. For most, reflection and introspection only follow a crisis, tragedy, or other significant emotional event. While reflection is certainly valuable in the aftermath of hardship, it's much more valuable when deployed as a ritual, as a routine and regular part of our life.

The Navy's Blue Angels debrief after every show to course correct and make adjustments before the next day's demonstration begins. In football, the offense huddles, runs a play, reconvenes in the huddle, and runs the next play. Both the Blue Angels and the football players will watch videos of their performances in order to determine what went well and where they can improve. After pinpointing mistakes, the succinct language used by Blue Angels to indicate improvement is, "I'll fix it." Videos add accountability; you can't hide from the film. These pre-planned strategic pauses build wisdom, improve performance, and reduce stress.

Here are three simple questions that I've been using to challenge entrepreneurs for almost twenty years. I can attest that, simple as they are, these questions draw invaluable ideas out of our own minds.

1. *What has been working?* In evaluating any situation, relationship, or timeframe, there are almost always some things that are working without a hitch or a hint of negativity. When reflecting, it's helpful to begin with the elements that are going well so that we keep a balanced perspective on the "big picture."

2. *What has not been working?* When we honestly assess any situation, we're able to identify at least a few things, large or small, that are giving us a little trouble, or not progressing the way we'd like. It's important that we acknowledge where we are missing the mark or have a weak spot so we can correct it before the next occurrence. Otherwise, the tendency is to keep doing things the same way.

3. *What do we need to improve?* This is the most important of the three questions because it translates our feedback into positive forward action. In light of our assessment of what's working and what's not, what do we need to do differently? How should we modify our strategy or change our approach so that we perform noticeably better next time?

We can use and benefit from these three questions in many different situations. We can use the questions at the end of the year, quarter, month, week, or day. When we debrief a whole year or quarter, we invest more time and thought than when we debrief a week, but the concept is the same. We can also use these questions to improve our performance after a meeting, a conversation, a date, or even a golf shot. These are also valuable questions to share with our children, as they force critical thinking and expand wisdom. Children and teenagers can learn to do a 60-second debrief of the important situations and activities they are involved in.

The Habit of Planning

We can learn from the past, but we can't improve it. We can no more change what happened this morning than we can change what happened in World War II. The influence we can have on our future, however, is almost unlimited. Planning is the deliberate act of pulling the future into the present, so we can do something about the future before it "happens to us." Planning really means evaluating our life in light of where we've been, where we are now, and where we intend to go. Planning reflects personal responsibility. In fact, it's one of the greatest responsibilities of any individual citizen. Planning has many valuable benefits:

- Encourages self-reliance
- Simplifies the complex
- Sharpens critical thinking
- Mitigates risk and uncertainty
- Requires and develops self-discipline
- Dissuades mediocrity

The presence of a thoughtful plan for our future indicates clearly that we're a serious participant in our own life. And the first step to planning is clarifying the end destination. A plan is just a list of action steps or directions for getting from our current location to a preferred location. Big, elaborate, highly-detailed plans can be valuable for certain goals, but a short, simple plan is always better than no plan at all.

First comes a better plan, and then comes a better life. If we want our future to be different, we must make things different in the present. Things rarely improve by themselves. Action without adequate planning is the cause of much frustration and the root of almost every failure. This is true for an individual, an organization, and a country. Just think how some quality planning ten years ago could have changed where our nation is today.

Day after day, year after year, individuals wake up and launch into frenetic activity with little or no vision of how their "to-do" list fits in with the rest of their life. As a coach, if someone tells me they're dissatisfied with some aspect of their life, I ask them bluntly, "What's your plan?" Whether they want to earn more money or have a better marriage, I ask the same question.

1. Do you want to lose weight? *What's your plan?*
2. Do you want to earn more money? *What's your plan?*
3. Do you want to invest more time with your kids? *What's your plan?*
4. Do you want to have a stronger marriage? *What's your plan?*
5. Do you want to influence the direction of this country? *What's your plan?*

Our plans should track back from the future. Where do we want to be at the end of our life? Where do we want to be at the end of next year? Where do we want to be at the end of next week? Where do we want to be tomorrow? Thomas Edison gives us one more reason to plan: "Good fortune is what happens when opportunity meets with planning."

The Habit of the Extra Mile

To be extraordinary, we have to give something *extra* to the world. We make ourselves unequal to the rest of the world by the way we lead our lives. This spirit is captured in a great saying: "If a man only does what is required of him, he is a slave—the moment he begins to do more than he is required, he becomes a free man."

The way capitalism works is a lot like being a server in a restaurant. Servers have an opportunity to earn a good tip. This is not an entitlement, just a possibility. Likewise, an entrepreneur, maybe the restaurateur in this case, has an opportunity to get wealthy. Again, there is no guarantee, just a possibility. Anything that the server can do to go the extra mile will increase the likelihood of a nice tip for himself, and more business for the restaurateur.

For the server to successfully draw a generous tip, he needs to provide the one-two punch of personality and performance while exceeding the expectations of the guest. This means the server needs to know the menu, understand the restaurant's operating system, be attentive but not intrusive, and develop a positive rapport with the potential tippers. If he does this, he'll receive a generous gratuity 95 percent of the time.

For the restaurant owner to be successful, she must risk her capital, create a unique dining experience, offer good food at a price potential customers are willing to pay, and exceed expectations during each subsequent visit. Should she accomplish these objectives, she has a great shot, but still no guarantee, of reaching her financial goals. Anything that the restaurateur can do to travel that lonely second mile will improve her chances of becoming wealthy.

When we travel beyond the initial mile, our potential becomes unlimited. High character individuals are continuously looking for opportunities to exceed expectations. So to become great, if that's still permissible, first become a servant. Treat others as you would want to be treated if your positions were reversed. Practice this whether the other person does or does not. Be generous. Dedicate yourself and your life to the service of others. Constantly ask yourself how you can increase your service and contribution. Ask, "How can I triple my value to my boss, to my clients, to the marketplace, to my family?" Write it down. No one can do the minimum and reach the maximum.

Every American needs to know that doing more than they are currently being paid for is the absolute fastest way to get paid *more* for what they do in the future. Bestselling author Brian Tracy calls it like it is: "Successful people are always looking for opportunities to help others. Unsuccessful people are always asking, 'What's in it for me?'"[9] And as Sam Walton advised, "Exceed your customer's expectations. If you do, they'll come back over and over. Give them what they want—and a little more. Let them know you appreciate them. Make good on all your mistakes, and don't make excuses—apologize. Stand behind everything you do."[10]

We should not have to apologize for more service and value to the marketplace, and consequently for reaping more rewards than the guy next door or the politician across town. Going the second mile, doing more than the minimum is a powerful habit for marriage, parenting, health, business, and every other area of our life.

The Habit of Intelligent Action

This is the habit of thinking, speaking, and behaving in a manner consistent with our desired destination. As simple as it sounds on the surface, this may be the most challenging habit to practice consistently. Since many choices are not preceded by intelligent thought, many actions seem quite foolish.

We've been blessed with the faculty of reason for the purpose of taking intelligent actions. But are we using this faculty? Earl Nightingale explains:

> To the exact extent that a person uses the greatest gift on earth, the gift of reasoning—of thinking—which belongs to him alone of all the creatures of the earth, will he determine the kind of environment in which he will live. Only man can make the scenery change to match him.
>
> By changing himself, he changes his surroundings. If a person understands this he understands, at the same time, why he is king over everything else. Because of this, he solves the riddles of the invisible germs; travels with the speed of two hundred hurricanes; swims to the bottom of the sea; and will one day visit the farthest planets of the universe.
>
> And yet, it is here where we find the greatest paradox: With this greatest gift of all, the great majority of people neither know they have it, nor use it, but spend most of their time aping those about them—playing a silly kind of copycat game that you'd expect to see in a tribe of baboons cavorting on the forest floor. No two of them are exactly alike, and yet they pretend they are, and they let a handful of their brothers do their thinking for them. Each of them has been given the greatest gift on earth and he doesn't even open the box.[11]

We live in a world where so many have in fact become educated beyond their intelligence. This means "book smart but street foolish," or the absence of good, old-fashioned horse sense. Even more bluntly put, despite our academic credentials, we are all still quite capable of acting like idiots.

So, what defines intelligence? Is it I.Q.? Is it the college we attended and the degrees we received? Is it our grade point average? Maybe it's our ability to solve problems. Or is it our ability to develop and maintain healthy, productive relationships? This begs two key questions that are hopelessly interrelated:

First, "What defines intelligence?"

Second, "What defines stupidity?"

As I have devoted most of my adult life to coaching ambitious individuals to reach and exceed their goals, I've developed what I call the street-tested definitions of both intelligence and stupidity. Here they are:

Intelligence is a way of acting that moves us closer to the things we value and appreciate in our life.

Stupidity is a way of acting that distances us from the very things we desire and appreciate in our life.

If my goal is to lose ten pounds, and I sneak brownies into my mouth before I go to bed, I'm an idiot. If I want an awesome relationship with my wife but I never make time for her, I'm an idiot. If I want to experience financial freedom but I sink money into depreciating assets, I'm an idiot. We all need to acknowledge where we've been idiots. This goes for our nation as well. If we don't, there's no end in sight. Every so often we need to "Doctor-Phil-It," and just ask ourselves, "How's this working for me?"

The Urban Dictionary defines stupid as "someone who has to look up 'stupid' in the dictionary because they don't know what it means."[12] Ben Franklin had his own take on it, saying, "We are all born ignorant, but one must work hard to remain stupid." And Will Rogers quipped, "If stupidity got us into this mess, then why can't it get us out?" Obviously, Congress misconstrued Rogers's sarcasm as legitimate advice.

We have to accept that some people are unwilling and therefore cannot be helped. They just have a big case of dumb, or what might be more accurately labeled, "inoperable stupidity." Nobel Prize winning economist Friedrich Hayek wrote, "We shall not grow wiser before we learn that much that we have done was very foolish."[13] With freedom comes some degree of stupidity, and this goes for individual citizens and the government alike. There is no legislative fix for this—we just have to try to elect less stupid people to office.

There is one big catch to this habit of "intelligent action." If we don't know where we are headed, we cannot be certain which road to take or what actions truly are "intelligent." Think about how this relates to our country. If we haven't defined what kind of country we want America to be ten, twenty, or thirty years from now, how do we know whether the huge and unprecedented decisions we are making today are wise decisions? If we haven't defined what kind of life we want to be living in our sixties, then how do we know what we ought to be doing in our thirties and forties?

And now think about this on an individual level: if we haven't defined what kind of adults we want our children to grow up and become, then how do we know if our parenting approach is taking our kids where we really want them to go? If we haven't given much thought to the health we want to experience in our later years, then how committed will we be now to live accordingly? As baseball legend Mickey Mantle said, "If I knew I was going to live this long, I'd have taken better care of myself."

Half of my entrepreneurial clients report being very good students and attending excellent academic colleges. The other half report being average students and attending ordinary colleges. Today, the two groups' income, net worth, health, and overall quality of life seem to be indistinguishable. How is this possible? It's because the second group has mastered the habit of intelligent action.

To summarize, we are idiots to the degree that we identify a meaningful goal and then think, speak, or act in a manner that moves us further away from that goal. This applies to everyone, from a janitor to a Rhodes Scholar. On the flip side, we are geniuses to the degree that we pinpoint a worthy goal and then think, speak, and behave in a manner that moves us closer to that goal.

THE BILL OF RESPONSIBILITIES:
A COMMITMENT WORTH MAKING

The Founders instinctively understood the principles and habits outlined here. They knew that rights without responsibilities are self-destructive. They understood the utter foolishness and ultimate demise that would come from expecting something for nothing. But the War on Success seeks to decimate the American work ethic. Our current administration wants to undermine all the principles and habits that lead to independent, self-fulfilling lives. If people are hard-working, successful, and content, then there's not much demand for an oversized government to step in and "fix" their lives—which is exactly what Barack Obama and his allies aim to do.

We need to give citizens more responsibility, not more entitlements. So here's a start—a Bill of Responsibilities for the American people.

As citizens of the United States, we have the following responsibilities:

1. *Gratitude:* We are responsible for expressing appreciation for the extraordinary freedom we enjoy.
2. *Self-Reliance:* We are responsible for taking care of ourselves and our families.
3. *Citizenship:* We are responsible for learning and understanding the nature of free government and the principles and practices of liberty.

4. *Duty:* We are responsible for staying alert, for resisting and vigorously defending breaches in freedom's foundation.

5. *Service:* We are responsible for providing more value if we desire more rewards in life.

6. *Community:* We are responsible for investing our time, talent, and resources in our local community.

7. *Healthcare:* We are responsible for taking care of our own health, vitality, and wellness.

8. *Personal Economy:* We are responsible for learning and practicing sound money-management principles.

9. *Family:* We are responsible for raising independent, self-reliant, and virtuous children who become productive citizens.

10. *Attitude:* We are responsible for asking only for opportunity.

11. *Allegiance:* We are responsible for mastering the English language and placing love of country above our ethnicity and culture of origin.

12. *Maturity:* We are responsible for owning the consequences of our choices.

13. *Posterity:* We are responsible for passing the torch of liberty and individual freedom to future generations.

These responsibilities will put this nation back on the right track when we begin applying them to our own lives. Each of us is the president and chief executive of our own life. The buck stops with no one else. We are responsible for determining where we take our life and who we will take along for the ride. If something in our life is unsatisfactory, it's up to us to fix it. We control the finances and budgeting, the R&D, and the marketing and sales of our own personal enterprise.

Too many Americans have stopped looking within themselves. If *you* are willing to seize the initiative, *you* can achieve great success in America, not because of the government, but because of your character.

Success is in your hands—as well it should be.

Yes, YOU can!

CHAPTER TEN

LET'S ROLL!

"The budget should be balanced, the Treasury should be refilled, public debt should be reduced, the arrogance of officialdom should be tempered and controlled, and the assistance to foreign lands should be curtailed lest Rome become bankrupt. People must again learn to work, instead of living on public assistance."

—CICERO (55 BC)

WE'RE ON OUR OWN. The future of our republic is no longer the responsibility of the politicians. It's the responsibility of *we the people.*

It's about you and me. It's about our kids, our grandkids, and their children's children. Our future as well as theirs is in our hands. We are clearly at a turning point in our nation's history. We want to be successful, and we want America to remain exceptional. But responsible citizenship can no longer be a spectator sport.

Recall Ben Franklin's warning, "Make yourselves sheep and the wolves will eat you." Do we want to be known as the generation that let individual liberties fade into the "collective good"? Or do we want to be remembered as the generation that stood up, stood firm, and proudly declared, "NOT ON OUR WATCH!"

Over the last two decades working as a strategic coach for several thousand entrepreneurs, I've repeatedly seen individuals put their business lives on hold to face down crises ranging from health problems to dying family members to sick children. For example, facing a cancer diagnosis, one entrepreneur temporarily gave control of her entire company to a trusted subordinate. After all, she wisely reasoned, "What value is my business when my life is at stake?" This wake-up call was, no doubt, a game changer— or perhaps we should say, a life changer. I often remind my clients that their goals won't matter much if they lose their health. I ask them, "If you don't take care of your body, where will you live?"

The same is true for our nation. If we don't take care of our country, where will our children and grandchildren live? In the United States right now, we've been given a liberty-threatening diagnosis. And like the cancer-stricken businesswoman, we must press the pause button on some of our routines, responsibilities, and lifestyle comforts to address the catastrophe that looms in our near future if aggressive measures are not quickly adopted. What responsible person would ignore a cancer diagnosis, assume it will resolve itself, or simply let the disease ravage her body without a fight?

LIBERTY IN JEOPARDY

Time is running out. Now that we have clearly spotted trouble ahead, we must fight back against the architects of the War on Success who aim to "remake" our country into their own image, into something our Founding Fathers never envisioned. We must seize the opportunity to fight the forces that have undermined our nation's foundation and threatened its economic, cultural, and moral health. As the afflicted businesswoman observed, what value is the life we've worked for if our liberty is in jeopardy?

We can no longer deny the destructive growth of government in this country. Our national character is at risk of being lost forever or diluted beyond recognition. As prudent, patriotic, and grateful citizens, we must not vote "present" at this critical juncture in our nation's history. Now is the time to mobilize.

Over two centuries of progress is at risk. We must not surrender our roots, trudge sheepishly in conformity, or selfishly abdicate our responsibility to future generations. What we do at this moment in history will determine the future of this country and impact the rest of the world in countless ways. Our response will determine how we measure up with the greatest generation that paid the price for us. With a brash revolution against the founding ideals well underway, we must counterattack with common sense.

General Douglas MacArthur wrote, "I am concerned for the security of our great Nation; not so much because of any threat from without, but because of the insidious forces working from within." We must get focused, organized, and united against this enemy from within. Fortunately, we don't need patriotic citizens to shed their blood, but only to share their ideas, their time, and their influence to reclaim our future. We must be free of clutter and confusion, and be clear about what matters most and why.

We cannot let this moment slip. In order to win the battle against an overreaching and collectivist-minded administration, enough of us must be willing to heed the call, honor our heritage, and accept an inconvenient detour in service to our posterity. We must make our voice heard. To effectively fight back against the War on Success we must, as individuals and as a nation, get back to basics.

WHO DO WE PLAY FOR?

In the movie *Miracle*, depicting the 1980 Olympic hockey match between the United States and the USSR, Coach Herb Brooks seeks to bring out the best in a U.S. team that's clearly less talented than the competition. Early in the movie, Brooks, played by Kurt Russell, asks the players three questions: "What's your name, where are you from, and who do you play for?" Each player answers with his name, hometown, and college team. Fishing for a different answer, Brooks reminds them that the name on the front of the jersey—USA—"is a hell of a lot more important than the one on the back."

LET'S ROLL!

1. **Let's minimize platitudes** and maximize authentic principles.

2. **Let's override our feelings** and reactivate our reason and logic.

3. **Let's stop treating the symptoms** and address the root causes.

4. **Let's stop apologizing for our nation** and reclaim our patriotism.

5. **Let's stop thinking about the next election** and start thinking about the next generation.

6. **Let's bury experimental values** and renew our timeless virtues.

7. **Let's stop living in the past** and start planning for the future.

8. **Let's refuse to tolerate mediocrity** and demand high standards.

9. **Let's return the phony stimulus** and unleash the real stimulus—America's entrepreneurs.

10. **Let's reject self-serving "complexity"** and return to simplicity.

11. **Let's abandon political correctness** and speak the plain truth.

12. **Let's drop class warfare** and start fighting actual problems.

13. **Let's stop seeking global popularity** and seek what is right according to *our* values, *our* virtues, and *our* hard-won individual rights.

14. **Let's stop believing in big government** and reaffirm "in God we trust."

15. **Let's Roll!**

Five months before the Olympics, the United States ties the Norwegians in a scrimmage. Brooks is livid, knowing that the team was unfocused, with the players pointing out pretty girls in the stands while the game was still in progress. So after the game, much to the players' surprise and chagrin, Brooks has them line up for suicide drills while the fans are still exiting the arena. After each drill Coach Brooks intensely commands, "Again!... Again!...Again!" The players are collapsing and even vomiting with exhaustion, but Brooks insists, "Again...Again...Again!" The rink manager turns the lights off, but Brooks continues the drills. Even when his assistant coach refuses to blow the whistle, Brooks barks out, "Again!"

Finally, one player, Mike Eruzione, has an "a-ha" moment. Barely able to string his words together, he yells out, "Mike Eruzione! Winthrop, Massachusettes!" Coach Brooks then asks him, "Who do you play for?" and Eruzione responds, "I play for the United States of America!" To everyone's relief, Brooks replies, "That's all gentlemen."

Those of us in the private sector have to step up. Politicians have fed dependence to the poor, pillaged the wealthy, and choked the middle class. It doesn't have to be this way. We don't play for the Democrats or the Republicans, we certainly don't play for the United Nations, and we're not global citizens. We are American citizens. We earned this proud distinction. *We play for the United States of America.*

THE FOUNDING PILLARS

If we can't defend our virtues and principles, we'll default to popular values and trendy programs. If we don't know what we stand for, we're likely to fall for anything. Our kids especially need to be well informed about the hot issues of the day—from religion to politics and everything in between.

So let's recap the founding pillars of our nation as illuminated by the Framers of the Constitution. Our children and teenagers especially need to know these truths to counterbalance the distorted versions presented in many schools and on most college campuses. In order to defend our convictions, we need to know why we believe what we believe and why it matters.

The Founding Principles of a Successful Nation

1. The Founders created a *constitutional republic*, not a democracy. This means the president and lawmakers must govern within the limits and laws of the Constitution to ensure personal liberties are preserved. This representative government avoids the opposing extremes of either mob rule or totalitarianism. Remember that you pledge allegiance to the flag, "and to the republic for which it stands."

2. The Founders knew *rights are God-given* and therefore "inalienable." Our individual rights such as our life, our pursuit of happiness, our religious convictions, our property rights, and our right to govern ourselves are not granted by man but by "nature's God," and cannot be taken away by the government.

3. The Founders established *self-government*. Well aware of the dangers of an oppressive, centralized government, they wanted power kept as close to the people as possible.

4. The Founders envisioned a *virtuous and self-reliant citizenry*. They considered this to be a prerequisite for successful and lasting self-government. These Judeo-Christian virtues included honesty, prudence, courage, personal responsibility, private charity, service, hard work, and thrift.

5. The Founders created a *limited government* in order to minimize the reach and meddling of the federal government into the business of the states and matters of individual citizens.

6. The Founders orchestrated the *separation of powers* so that government authority is dispersed between the legislative, executive, and judicial branches. This was designed as a safeguard against tyranny.

7. The Founders promoted *free enterprise*, which means individual citizens voluntarily exchange goods and services without governmental interference. The prospect of profit drives innovation, supply, and quality. Prices are determined by competition, not centralized government planners and regulators.

8. The Founders insisted on the *sanctity of private property* by tasking the government with protecting individual property rights and enforcing contracts.

9. The Founders wanted *equal opportunity* for Americans, not equal outcomes. Every virtuous citizen was meant to have a shot at creating and experiencing their own version of the American Dream. Liberty, the Founders knew, breeds inequality of outcomes.

Relearning and teaching these basic principles will help bring about a Constitutional comeback for the nation. If this renewal doesn't happen, we're going to keep playing this big government game with no rulebook. And we've seen the sorry results that approach has produced in Europe and elsewhere.

A Constitution is much like a mission statement for a business. And entrepreneurs who ignore their mission statement almost always suffer the same maladies: inefficiency, waste, poor judgment, vacillation, acts of expediency, miscommunication, redundancy, underperformance, and frustration. That's a pretty dead-on description of our government today, a direct result of its disregard of constitutional principles.

When a client doesn't live by his mission statement, I tell him he's living a lie. I advise him to either start living in alignment with his mission or change it. As a nation, it's time we do the same. I'll make a bold proposition here: let's follow our Constitution or formally trash it. If it means nothing to our political leaders, why don't we get rid of it? Wouldn't that be a more honest approach than formally retaining it while flagrantly ignoring it in practice?

BECOME PART OF THE SOLUTION

If we choose to once again adhere to the Constitution, we need to take some concrete steps to revitalize its principles in our own lives. The action steps below will get you off the sideline and onto the playing field where you can make a difference. Scan the list and identify the initiatives that strike a chord with you, that will enable you to become part of a rejuvenated and "spirited citizenry."

- *Question what every policy proposal means to your personal liberties and to those of your fellow citizens.* Few policies today are liberty-neutral. They either increase individual freedom or decrease it. Examine critically both the motives behind all proposed legislation and the likely consequences. What might be the *unintended* consequences? Does this pull us away from the Founders' principles or closer to them? Does it bolster the individual or build up the state? Does it reward and incentivize success or does it penalize it?
- *Take the pledge of independence.* Here's a short vow to get you focused: "I hereby accept total responsibility for my life and promise to pay in full and in advance

the price demanded for the lifestyle I desire. If I'm dissatisfied with any aspect of my life, I don't blame or complain; instead, I take constructive action to improve it. I eradicate all resentment and envy toward those doing "better" than I am. I refuse government handouts or financial benefits of any kind. This is how I choose to live my life from this day forth."

- *Filter your giving.* Become selective about the people and organizations to whom you donate money. Ironically, the socialist movement is funded in large part by generous capitalists. Socialist-leaning and other anti-American causes are buried within some seemingly benign organizations, foundations, and even churches that all rely on private donations.

  Business should stop funding anti-business causes. This is particularly true in the academic arena. Freeze all giving until you are confident that your hard-earned funds will not be utilized for socialist or other unpatriotic projects and agendas. If necessary, earmark your funds for specific areas, such as math, science, and athletics, which are less likely to be corrupted.

- *Drop PC, go PT.* Become part of the *Patriotic Movement.* This comprises all Americans who speak respectfully and gratefully about their nation's heritage. It's also the *Plain Talking Movement* of saying what we mean and meaning what we say. It's polite, respectful, and dignified, but it's also direct and courageous, never willing to bend a knee to PC pieties.

  We can no longer afford to shade the truth beneath the euphemisms of political correctness. We need thicker skin but a thinner handbook of speech etiquette. Stop being intimidated by the PC culture, and follow the strategy laid out by Charlton Heston for resisting it:

"You simply disobey. Peacably, yes. Respectfully, of course. Nonviolently, absolutely. But when told how to think or what to say or how to behave, we don't. We disobey the social protocol that stifles and stigmatizes personal freedom."[1]

Granted, we never should have let it go this far, but better late than never! Enough is enough. Take the muzzle off. Reject group-think. Think for yourself and teach your kids to do the same. The future of our republic depends on turning today's teenagers into wise, independent thinkers. Teach them to reject "diversity" that suppresses critical thinking, demands uniform speech, or censors contrarian views. Talk to your kids' teachers and read your kids' textbooks to find out what they're learning about American history. Whenever necessary, give them the other side of the story.

As I mentioned earlier, the truth is no less true simply because some may find it objectionable. We need to talk publicly about the issues of our day without being hypersensitive about different perspectives. Remember, unless plain speaking is allowed, clear thinking is denied.

- *Cultivate a "success culture" in your home.* Speak highly around the dinner table about the successful people in your community and throughout the country, across all fields of endeavor. Learn and teach our founding principles to your children and grandchildren; they are virtually synonymous with success. Courses presented by The National Center for Constitutional Studies and other organizations are popping up around the country. Take advantage of these opportunities to learn the Founders' original intent for our nation and how their principles are still relevant today.

You can also assign your own summer reading. Have your kids read books about great leaders, self-reliant difference makers, and our Founding Fathers. Share the principles of success. Identify the virtues you want to see come alive in their character.

- *Get out and stay out of personal debt.* We live in a time when people are spending what they don't have, to buy what they don't need, to impress people they don't even like. The solution here is easy: stop it. As Calvin Coolidge said, "There is no dignity quite so impressive, and no one independence quite so important, as living within your means."

- *Reject identity politics.* Always think of yourself as an American, first and foremost—not a hyphenated American, just a good, old-fashioned, patriotic American.

- *Talk to your kids about socialism.* Use academic, athletic, family, or household-based examples and metaphors to illustrate the false promises of socialist ideology. Discuss socialism's abysmal global track record throughout history. Explain that capitalism is voluntary and socialism is compulsory.

- *Explain your children's future debt.* Explain the national debt to your children, and that each of them will owe in excess of six figures once they enter the workforce. Visit www.usdebtclock.org with the whole family and bookmark it as a favorite site. If your college-aged teenager is enamored by "hope and change," patiently explain how much it all really costs—and that it's going to come out of his future income. While you're at it, explain the looming bankruptcy of Social Security.

THE SIMPLE FIVE DAY PLAN

The War on Success is advanced, but it's not too late to stop it. Here are five simple steps you can take in less than a week to counteract it.

- *Day One:* Create your patriot network, an email distribution list of at least five other responsible citizens, to have handy for sharing information, updates, helpful books, and facts about what is truly happening in our federal government on a week to week basis.
- *Day Two:* Use the Internet to locate the phone numbers, fax numbers, office addresses, and email addresses of your congressmen and senators. Copy and keep this information in a digital document or other convenient spot, and email it to others in your district. Then turn on the pressure whenever Congress votes on the next government takeover.
- *Day Three:* Write a letter to your children, grandchildren, or future children about why the American Dream is worth defending. This will clarify your own convictions, inspire your children (sooner or later), and motivate yourself to stand firm on what matters most. Use ideas from this book if that helps. Several real-life letters are reproduced in Appendix 1.
- *Day Four:* Join or sponsor the Heritage Foundation, FreedomWorks, or one of the other influential limited-government organizations identified in Appendix 2. Formally becoming a part of these organizations costs little, but gets you plugged in to expert analysis and provides resources for you to email to your patriot network.
- *Day Five:* Join a local or national tea party group and make a commitment to attend one upcoming event.

Learn more from a site like www.teapartypatriots.org.
Bring your children with you and invite your patriot list
to join you at the next event.

POLITICAL INITIATIVES

We need to think outside the box to develop new political policies
that reverse our steady slide into big-government statism. The following are a few such ideas. We don't all need to agree on them,
but simply debating them will push the national conversation in a
good direction—away from mega-plans for new government programs and toward small-government solutions that enhance individual freedom.

- *Unleash the entrepreneurs.* Our government's number
  one goal after national security should be to stimulate
  entrepreneurial activity. Let's remove all roadblocks
  and speed bumps that weaken the ambition and slow
  the innovation of our secret weapon—American business. Stop the demonizing rhetoric, minimize interference, streamline regulations, and lower taxes. If our
  leaders did this, it would quickly become the greatest
  stimulus package ever.

  To further improve the business climate, slash or
  even eliminate corporate taxes, which are either directly
  or indirectly passed on to consumers anyway. We
  should also drastically reduce or eliminate capital gains
  taxes, and at all costs, we must defeat attempts to
  approve new energy taxes in the hidden form of a "cap-
  and-trade" carbon trading scheme.

  While we're at it, let's pass the nonpartisan Fair Tax
  Act (HR 25, S 296). This would replace the entire
  federal tax system with an integrated approach

comprising a progressive national retail sales tax, a pre-
bate to ensure no one pays federal taxes on spending up
to the poverty level, dollar-for-dollar federal revenue
neutrality, and, through companion legislation, the
repeal of the Sixteenth Amendment, which allows the
government to levy a federal income tax.

The Fair Tax would abolish the following kinds of
taxes: federal, personal, and corporate income, gift,
estate, capital gains, alternative minimum, Social Security, Medicare, and self-employment. Instead, we'd
have one simple, transparent, federal retail sales tax
administered primarily by existing state sales tax
authorities. It would tax us only on what we choose
to spend on new goods or services, not on what we
earn. The Fair Tax is a fair, efficient, and intelligent
solution to the frustration and inequity of our current
tax system.[2]

- *Stop the presses.* Printing money to cover budget short-
falls debases the dollar and stokes the hidden inflation
tax. It's a mechanism for more subtly manipulating the
wealth and private property attained by hard working
Americans. We should only print money to replace
existing money.

- *Remove all incumbents.* We have to stop voting for the
problem creators. Let's get rid of the professional politicians and return to the concept of citizen legislators.
After they serve a few terms, we should force politicians
to return to the real world and produce something of
value, not simply supervise the distribution of other
people's hard-earned money.

In the 2010 elections, let's all work together to fire
the chronic politicians and elect statesmen who are
more concerned with the next generation than the next

election cycle. If private sector employees approved a fraction of the spending Congress has without even reading where the money is going, they'd be fired and escorted out by security.

The downside of term limits is that we'll doubtless lose a few wise, responsible, elected officials. But they'll probably do more good in the private sector anyway.

- *Stop automatic withholding of projected taxes.* This was supposed to be a temporary policy to help fund the war effort during World War II. But inevitably, as is the case with nearly every big government program, the scheme rocks on indefinitely. More precisely, we the people have *allowed* this to continue. Automatic tax deductions enable higher taxes by removing the shock of writing a single check to the IRS for our annual tax bill. If everyone realized how much their income tax really is, there'd be a lot more pressure to let us keep the money we've earned.

  And here's another idea: since everyone will have to pay their taxes on one day, why don't we make it the day before Election Day?

- *Allow children to vote.* All right, this proposal might not get very far. But think about it—if our children's future is being mortgaged, shouldn't they have a say in the decisions? The rationale for banning kids from voting is that they're ignorant of the issues and aren't emotionally mature, but that argument doesn't impress me—by that logic most politicians today shouldn't be voting either.

- *Expand the income tax.* Nearly half the people don't pay any federal income tax at all. Until we pass the Fair Tax, we should expand the income tax so that everyone contributes to the country's tax coffers, even if it's just a small amount. Otherwise, those paying no taxes have no direct incentive to slow the growth of government. Let's make sure everyone has some skin in the game.

■ *Balance the budget by shrinking the government.* Since taxes are already too high, the only way to balance the budget is to cut government spending. The reason waste and inefficiency mar so many big-government programs is because the government is doing too many things it was never intended to do. In their wisdom and foresight, the Founders tried to restrain the size of government. They knew a bloated national government would become either inefficient, corrupt, or both.

We'd all do well to heed the advice of former Chrysler CEO Lee Iacocca, who said, "One of the things the government can't do is run anything. The only things our government runs are the post office and the railroads, and both of them are bankrupt." It also runs Social Security, Medicare, and Medicaid, which are all effectively broke or teetering on insolvency. But that didn't stop the government from taking over General Motors or numerous financial firms, or from greedily eyeing other vulnerable targets like failing newspapers. Oh yeah, and it's on the brink of taking over healthcare—one-sixth of the economy.

■ *Promote honorable private charities.* Private charities tend to be good stewards of the money they disperse. Otherwise, they don't stay in operation very long. They don't have the coercive power of the federal government at their disposal, so they recognize they're using other people's hard-earned money. People wouldn't keep giving money to charities that have squandered it in the past. Charitable organizations have to earn their donations by selling their good cause to benefactors and then investing the money wisely to maintain future opportunities and cultivate a good reputation. The federal government is neither concerned with "selling its cause" or maintaining a great reputation, since it forcibly extracts our money regardless of its past performance.

- *Promote independence for the poor.* Let's really help the poor and those in need. We can start by distinguishing between the deserving and undeserving poor. With the current welfare system, there is no exit plan, no long-term help, just the promise of free money with the perpetual reaffirmation of victimhood. We need to raise our standards, stop helping the needy just to cope, and start helping them to achieve, succeed, and thrive.

Welfare recipients should receive a schedule of diminishing benefits and be obliged to present evidence showing a good-faith effort to find work. If they're capable of providing something in exchange for what they're receiving, then they should be required to do so, even if the contribution is minimal. The chronically unemployed should have to serve the community in some way. Require something, anything, in exchange for their checks.

Welfare, or government-based charity, fails largely because it addresses the symptoms of poverty, not the root causes that lie in the choices many people have made. Economics professor Walter Williams identifies these choices in his sensible advice on "how not to be poor." He writes, "Avoiding long-term poverty is not rocket science. First, graduate from high school. Second, get married before you have children, and stay married. Third, work at any kind of job, even one that starts out paying the minimum wage. And, finally,

avoid engaging in criminal behavior."[3] This is common
sense for sure, but not common practice, and certainly
not something that politicians have the guts to discuss
publicly.

A final reform to improve welfare would be to cut
D.C. out of the picture entirely and put the onus on
states and local governments. Instead of a distant, massive, faceless, centralized bureaucracy, the programs
would be run by local representatives more intimately
connected to their communities.

- *Overpay if you like.* We should provide all citizens who
  support high taxes, transfer payments, and other redistribution schemes with an easy method for sending
  more of their own cash to the government when they
  file their taxes. The IRS could put a check box on every
  form under the header: *Check here to acknowledge we
  know better how to spend your money.* The taxpayer
  could then indicate the additional amount he is sub-
  mitting to the treasury.

WHAT IS OUR DESTINY?

Only a few months after he was sworn in as 44th President of the
United States, Barack Obama was asked in Europe if he believed
in American exceptionalism. He said he did—in the same way
that "the Brits believe in British exceptionalism and the Greeks
in Greek exceptionalism."[4] Of course, that was just a long way
of saying "no." Coming from the president, that answer was
unacceptable.

America is an exceptional country, and Americans are a special
people. We have become the world's preeminent military and economic power, its chief guarantor of free trade and international
security, and its biggest advocate for democracy. We have gotten

OBAMA VS. FOUNDERS

OBAMA'S VISION	FOUNDERS' VISION
Government Dependence	Self-reliance
Charity must be forced	Voluntary Charity
Something for nothing	Something for something
Reap what others sow	Reap what you sow
Pursuit of security	Pursuit of happiness
Equal outcomes	Equal opportunity
Rights come from state	Rights come from God
Self-betterment not needed	Self-betterment expected
All work is valuable	Valuable work is valuable
Rewards intention and effort	Rewards results
Celebrates mediocrity	Celebrates excellence
Government-run business and intervention	Free markets
Follows international community	No entangling alliances
High taxes	Low taxes
Big government	Limited government
Global citizenship	U.S. citizenship
Secular society	God-centered society
Values community over individual	Values individual over community
Globalization	Patriots
International values come first	U.S. values come first
Tolerance among citizenry	Virtue among citizenry
Diversity regardless of performance	Performance regardless of diversity
E pluribus pluribus (Diversity)	*E pluribus unum* (Unity)

where we are not through luck or coincidence, but by adhering to a system of law, economics, and government founded more than 200 years ago on Judeo-Christian values.

Those values are now under attack. With the War on Success, longstanding American freedoms are at risk of compromise and dilution. And as John Adams wrote, "Liberty once lost is lost forever." So we must decide: is success worth fighting for? Is America's future worth the fight?

If we are defeated, we will lose the liberty that we have come to take for granted. We will lose the opportunity that inspired us. We will lose our dreams of success. And so will our children and their children. As a nation, we will lose our very identity. And the unmatched attractiveness, distinctiveness, and effectiveness of this nation will fade into a blended and commoditized world culture.

That is not the vision for which countless American veterans have sacrificed. From the Revolutionary War to the present day, Americans soldiers put their lives on the line to defend liberty and to keep Americans safe from tyranny. Our brave soldiers have not fought throughout history for statist and socialist dogma—they have fought against it. They have not risked their lives on faraway battlefields so they could return home to a listless, regimented nation crushed by the overwhelming demands and diktats of a leviathan government. As veteran after veteran from across the country has passionately told me, "I did not risk my life for socialism." Our great military has fought for our founding ideals: life, liberty, and the pursuit of happiness—not mediocrity, collectivism, and government-guaranteed happiness.

The War on Success is a war we can win. It's a war we must win. Now is the time to act. Truth, history, and principle are on our side. We have accomplished too much to leave a legacy of lost liberty to our children and grandchildren. As Thomas Paine wrote, "A generous parent would have said, 'If there must be trouble, let it be in my day, that my child may have peace.'"[5]

While Barack Obama wrote eloquently about the dreams from his father, his policies are creating nightmares for our children and grandchildren. John Adams wrote, "Posterity, you will never know how much it cost the present generation to preserve your freedom. I hope you will make good use of it. If you do not, I shall repent in heaven that ever I took half the pains to preserve it." Those who seek to break the bond of our first principles must not be allowed to frame the debate. It is no longer satisfactory for us simply to defend the cause of individual freedoms; we must become the champions of it. Our patriotic duty is to intelligently confront, debate, and defeat bad ideas.

Traditionally, the most effective activists and protestors have been those looking for goodies from the government. With time on their hands to organize, march, and make demands, they have become proficient at panhandling for government favors. Unfortunately, successful people from all walks of life usually work long hours and don't have time to be political activists. And conservatives in particular are rarely activists—they prefer to mind their own business, earn their own living, and spend leftover time with family and friends. So up until now, we have relied on our elected officials to represent and defend the cause of freedom and the cause of individual success.

This must change. We can no longer abdicate our fight to professional politicians. We need to organize, march, protest, and agitate—not to get free stuff, but to get *free-dom*—to get the government off our backs and out of the way. Passivity, at this moment, is unacceptable. No more sitting around, moaning and groaning. Let's do something huge. Let's put the pressure on!

The template for action has already been established by the tea party protestors, who show us how to get involved and get our voices heard. In your own community, join with likeminded people and hit the streets. Protest the Obama administration's out-of-control spending and our nation's slide into statist mediocrity.

Be ready to articulate your points respectfully but firmly in case you are interviewed by the press. Confront your elected representatives about their votes—and if you don't get satisfactory answers, support challengers who will defend the free market and stand up for merit. And if you can't find a good challenger, think about running for office yourself.

Like the heroes of Flight 93, we must launch into action. We need to thwart the efforts to remake this nation into something the Founders never envisioned. We must rise to the occasion and resist the bloated government excesses that will rob this country of its greatness.

We are at a defining moment, a turning point that will shape the rest of our lives and those of our children. We must get out of the stands and onto the field where we can influence the game that's being played with our future and our posterity. We must refuse to lose this fight. We must refuse to abandon the principles that brought our country this far, elevated our aspirations, and created unprecedented leaps in prosperity. We must refuse to go along with the crowd just so we can get along. Doing what is popular is often not the right thing to do. Isn't this what we tell our children?

Popular or not, we must marshal all our creative energy to stall the stubborn advance of socialism and the vices that accompany it—apathy, dependence, and averageness. We cannot afford to experiment with the camouflaged, recycled, and disproven theories of social engineering. If America is to regain its greatness, it will not be through government programs, but through the people's demand that we return to our founding principles.

As American citizens, we have the right to equal opportunity, not equal outcomes. We have the freedom to succeed and also the freedom to fail. We have the right to make the choices in our lives we believe will make us happy. If we make wise choices, then we have the right to enjoy the fruits of those choices. If we end up making bad choices, then we must suffer the consequences.

Fortunately, we also have the right to learn from our mistakes and make better choices in the future. We have the option of sacrificing our time or money in hopes of earning a bigger reward. We have the right to plan more, read more, learn more, work more, practice more, risk more, and become more than the average person. We can exercise our equal opportunity to become unequal—to become more successful, more wealthy, or more happy by any other measure—or we can choose to be average, or even something less. This is the American way!

There is no time to waste. Today is the day. Today presents the opportunity to stand up, push back, and influence the decisions that are being made on our behalf. It won't be easy. But, as Thomas Paine still cheers us on, "These are the times that try men's souls. The summer soldier and the sunshine patriot will, in this crisis, shrink from the service of their country, but he that stands it now, deserves the love and thanks of man and woman. Tyranny, like hell, is not easily conquered; yet we have this consolation with us, that the harder the conflict, the more glorious the triumph."[6]

We can no longer sit back and rely on the government to make things right. America's greatness depends on "WE THE PEOPLE." America's greatness depends on you.

Let's Roll!

ACKNOWLEDGMENTS

FIRST AND FOREMOST, my deepest gratitude goes to my wife Kristin and my three sons for changing their summer and fall plans to accommodate my writing schedule, and for putting up with a husband and dad who was often in close physical proximity but was positively preoccupied for five months.

Special thanks to my chief collaborator, Hunter Hill, who shared his brain and invested many of his evenings, early mornings, and weekends brainstorming with me and helping me fine-tune the message of the book.

Thank you, Elizabeth Irvin, for relentlessly digging up, sorting, prioritizing, and summarizing the speeches, facts, history, and other background material that made this book a reality. Thanks also to David Wright for his very helpful research as the writing got underway.

I am grateful for my assistant Shelly Guberman for keeping me, my research, and my early drafts organized while keeping the rest of *The 1% Club* office running smoothly.

Thanks to my Mastermind group for challenging me to get out of my comfort zone, follow my calling, and "just do it"—and with their help, I did. Thanks to Ryan Cone, Ron Raitz, Joe Hamilton, Sid Johnson, Mike Ivey, Mark Seeley, and Bradley Fulkerson.

A number of very special people encouraged me or challenged me through the process, possibly without even realizing it, including: Dave Armento, Frank Bell, Mike Campbell, Judy Crawford, Jeff Kemp, Matthew Spalding, Mark Crawford, Tom Elias, Scott Barron, Ed McCrady, Jan Taylor, Ernest Taylor, Darren Fink, and Randy Walton. Thanks in particular to Bruce Boring for your one-of-a-kind encouragement that kept me from almost passing on this project.

Thank you, Curt Beavers, for your commitment to making principles matter most!

Thank you to Dr. Michael Youssef and Craig Snyder for your insights into socialism and the scriptures.

I am grateful for the entrepreneurs and business leaders from across the country who shared their insights and perspectives about the American Dream. I appreciate everyone who sent me articles, notes, and stories that added to my perspective.

Thanks to my agent, Pamela Harty at The Knight Agency, for pushing me to get this project into a proposal and ready for the market.

Thanks to Marji Ross, Mary Beth, and the great team at Regnery for catching the vision; to the Regnery publicity and marketing folks for their fantastic efforts to spread word of this book far and wide; and to my editor, Jack Langer, who continually polished the ideas into a manuscript that will mobilize readers to stand up for timeless principles and traditional values.

Finally, infinite gratitude to my parents for believing in me, and to God for nudging me to put my convictions in writing.

APPENDIX 1

The War on Success aims to snuff out the American Dream that has inspired millions of immigrants and native-born Americans alike. To fully convey what's at stake, I sponsored the American Dream Letter Writing Campaign, which invited participants to write letters to their children and grandchildren about the American Dream. The following heartfelt letters simply and beautifully express the significance of the American Dream and why it's worth fighting for.

Dear Emma and Katherine,

As we discuss during our ride to school most mornings, I am deeply concerned at the current direction of our nation. I am convinced that continuing our present path will lead to certain financial ruin for this country. The continually increasing intrusion of government into our daily lives, the vilification of successful (and happy) individuals, and the erosion of personal responsibility will lead us to further devalue personal success and effort and excellence.

However, I want to share with you my hope for you and indeed for our nation. As we have also discussed exhaustively, your grandfather began life on a rural farm that can only be described as primitive. In fact, I can recall in one my earliest memories my father and uncles installing running water (read: a bathroom) in

---

You can read more American Dream letters at www.thewaronsuccess.com. To submit your own letter, email a copy to americandream@thewaronsuccess.com.

my grandparents' farm house. The family raised most of their food, made most of their clothes, and had only a radio to keep up with events outside their "small world." I can also remember their first TV with 2 channels!

They were a fiercely independent family and valued this independence more than I can describe. They lived simply. And at the risk of resorting to an overused cliché, the children truly walked many miles to school each day, regardless of the weather. They returned home to help with the innumerable chores and work required of farm life.

What is instructive is that each of the children grew up to find success as entrepreneurs and professionals. While only one graduated from college (law degree from Northwestern University), the others together started several businesses and found their definition of success in a hardscrabble rural economy. My father started with surplus WWII equipment and little capital and built one of the most admirable companies in the area. He was known to everyone as hardworking, diligent, independent, and industrious. (So industrious that my father and uncle built, from scratch, the first school bus in our poor county.)

With no help (and little intrusion) from the government, he created an enterprise providing employment to many people whose only job options can be described as dismal. The opportunity to work for his company was valued and viewed as a step to a better life in a tough place. He created for his employees both a positive environment and a path leading to a better life.

I am certain that the only place this story can be told is in America. There is no system other than free enterprise where someone of little resources can, through persistence and freedom, create a better life for their family, employees, and themselves. The system that led this nation to become the world's strongest, most influential, and dominant economy in only 130 years makes the story of my father and his family possible. This country's success story is made up of my family's journey experienced by countless others in a different time and place.

So while I am discouraged by the national mood at the moment, I know this too shall pass. I firmly believe that our country will again discover the miracle of small, independent business. If I did not have faith in the underlying principles that have guided this country, I would not work and sacrifice as I do. And I know that with the same hard work and long-term perspective, you too will find happiness, success, and significance. You too will have an opportunity to create a better environment and opportunity for yourself and others. You too will be able to enjoy the satisfaction of creating something of significance that makes this country a better place and furthers its potential.

—Dad

Dear Nicholas,

This is being written as a part of the American Dream Campaign and is meant to share my thoughts as to the opportunities presented to us because of the freedoms we enjoy as Americans. As you are well aware, these freedoms are the results of much forethought, bravery, and effort on the part of the country's Founding Fathers, as well as the sacrifices made by countless others through wars, economic turmoil, and political unrest.

Though these opportunities are available, it is up to you to take advantage of them . . . to decide what you want to achieve, accomplish, and create. As George Bernard Shaw said, "People are always blaming where they are in life on circumstance. I don't believe in circumstances. Those who get on in this world are those who find the circumstances they want. And if they don't find them, they create them."

Your grandfather is a living example of this. Having grown up poor in Florence, AL, he enlisted in the Marines for WWII, fought his way through the Pacific, and returned with a new sense of determination; that is, he determined he would be successful. After graduating from college, he began creating his career. Soon, unsatisfied with his circumstances, he created his own by starting his own company. He went on to distinguish himself and become a leader in his field. But nothing was given or expected. He earned it through planning, hard work, and sacrifice.

Others like him, these members of the "greatest generation," create an example and legacy for us to follow: that your future really is up to you. No excuses, no blame. It will be built on your personal commitment to your dream. It will not be easy and there will be numerous obstacles. Will you have the grit and determination to overcome them? Will you see the obstacles for what they are—opportunities that will stop others and allow you to separate and prove yourself? Will you demand yourself to fully develop the talents and abilities God has given you and refuse to fall short of your dreams? Will you create the circumstance you want, rather than accepting and settling for those put in your path?

Truly, your future is up to you. You are in a country that, despite those who seek to socialize our achievements, still rewards individual excellence. It is up to you. What future will you create?

With much love and hope,
Dad

Dear Jason, Alex, and Carson,

The land in Texas that you both love so dearly, the land you have spent most all holidays and birthdays of your life, was a gift to you by your great-great-grandfather. He and your grandfather were such great examples of men who lived the American Dream. My prayer for both of you is that you come to understand how these men became the success stories they were and that you will become passionate in your adult life about maintaining these core values that have made men like them and this country strong.

Your great-great grandfather was a stowaway on a ship from Germany in the early 1880s. Galveston, Texas, was still a big seaport then (prior to the Hurricane of 1900 which devastated the city). He settled in Austin County, worked hard, and from nothing at all, eventually made enough money to start buying up land. He farmed and built his house in the mid-1880s and yes, you know the rest of the story—that is our house! The 500 acres we now enjoy just an hour west of Houston were bought by your penniless German ancestor.

Your grandfather, my dad, was cut from the same cloth. He finished 8th grade and then set out to work. When he retired in 1973 as a welder, he had amassed quite a nest egg from the variety of entrepreneurial ventures he had successfully completed during his lifetime. He became a solid upper middle classer and frequently vacationed back in Europe where this story all started.

What made these two men successful? Mostly, they weren't afraid of hard work and even less afraid of taking risk. During their lifetimes, the United States was a country made for men like them who worked hard, took risks, and sometimes amassed huge fortunes. These men (the oilmen) owed the Gulf Coast region a lot, and they collectively repaid the city with millions of charitable dollars for the arts, science, humanities, medicine, and NASA.

Unfortunately, our country seems to have forgotten how we got here. Hard work is no longer honored as much—we now believe everyone is "owed" a good life, whether they are willing to work or not. We have somehow grown to believe that everything we have is owed to us—nothing is a privilege, but expected. We have lived the "good life" and now we have come to expect it. We aren't a proud people any longer because we haven't really "earned" what we have.

Our morals, our values, and our core beliefs are all compromised. We have become a nation that is afraid to take risks, we want instant success without much work, and we have become so afraid of not being "tolerant" that we're afraid to take a stand on anything, even our most core beliefs.

I believe that your generation has become so brainwashed that to be "tolerant" you must accept other people's ideals, that no one really has any ideals any longer. You don't trust people who take action quickly and you don't believe in certainty. My prayer for both of you is that you don't fall into this trap of relativism. My prayer is that God will give you discernment and that you will see His example of Truth in every decision you make. My prayer for you is that you will grow to be strong men of God who are sensitive to people and their needs, but men who are willing to take a stand for what you believe.

You have a strong heritage, and this country has a strong heritage. Please don't let either slip away.

> Love you more than you'll ever know,
> Mom

A PATRIOT'S RESOURCE GUIDE

TV

- Fox News: www.foxnews.com
- Fox Business: www.foxbusiness.com
- Kudlow & Company (CNBC): www.kudlow.com
- Morning Joe (MSNBC): www.msnbc.msn.com

RADIO

- Bill Bennett: www.bennettmornings.com
- Dave Ramsey: www.daveramsey.com
- Dennis Prager: www.dennisprager.com
- Glenn Beck: www.glennbeck.com
- Hugh Hewitt: www.hughhewitt.townhall.com/blog
- Laura Ingraham: www.lauraingraham.com
- Mark Levin: www.marklevinshow.com
- Mike Gallagher: www.mikeonline.com

- Michael Medved: www.michaelmedved.com
- Michael Reagan: www.reagan.com
- Neal Boortz: www.boortz.com
- Radio America: www.radioamerica.org
- Rush Limbaugh: www.rushlimbaugh.com
- Sean Hannity: www.hannity.com
- Salem Radio Network: www.srnonline.com

BOOKS

- *The 5000 Year Leap*, Cleon Skousen
- *Arguing with Idiots*, Glenn Beck
- *As a Man Thinketh*, James Allen
- *Catastrophe*, Dick Morris
- *Culture of Corruption*, Michelle Malkin
- *FairTax: The Truth: Answering the Critics*, Neal Boortz and John Linder
- *Liberty & Tyranny*, Mark Levin
- *Principle of the Path*, Andy Stanley
- *Real Change*, Newt Gingrich
- *Saving Freedom*, Jim DeMint
- *The Science of Success*, Charles Koch
- *Something for Nothing*, Brian Tracy
- *Success Is Not an Accident*, Tommy Newberry
- *They Think You're Stupid*, Herman Cain
- *We Still Hold These Truths*, Matthew Spalding

MAGAZINES & NEWSPAPERS

- *American Spectator*: www.spectator.org
- *Forbes*: www.forbes.com

- *Human Events*: www.humanevents.com
- *Investor's Business Daily*: www.investors.com
- *National Review*: www.nationalreview.com
- *Wall Street Journal*: www.wsj.com
- *Washington Times*: www.washingtontimes.com
- *Weekly Standard*: www.weeklystandard.com
- *WORLD Magazine*: www.worldmag.com

WEBSITES & BLOGS

- The Corner at National Review Online: corner.nationalreview.com
- Drudge Report: www.drudgereport.com
- Free Republic: www.freerepublic.com
- Herman Cain: www.hermancain.com
- Hot Air: www.hotair.com
- Instapundit: www.instapundit.com
- Mark Steyn: www.steynonline.com
- Media Research Center: www.mediaresearch.org
- Michelle Malkin: www.michellemalkin.com
- Newsbusters: www.newsbusters.org
- Newsmax: www.newsmax.com
- Porkbusters: www.porkbusters.org
- Powerline: www.powerlineblog.com
- Real Clear Politics: www.realclearpolitics.com
- Red State: www.redstate.com
- Right Wing News: www.rightwingnews.com
- Say Anything: www.sayanythingblog.com
- Townhall: www.townhall.com
- World Net Daily: www.worldnetdaily.com

ORGANIZATIONS AND THINK TANKS

- Accuracy in Media: www.aim.org
- American Conservative Union: www.conservative.org
- American Enterprise Institute: www.aei.org
- Cato Institute: www.cato.org
- Center for Freedom and Prosperity: www.freedomandprosperity.org
- Center for Responsive Politics: www.opensecrets.org
- Center for Security Policy: www.centerforsecuritypolicy.org
- Competitive Enterprise Institute: www.cei.org
- Eagle Forum: www.eagleforum.org
- Family Policy Council: www.citizenlink.org
- Federalist Society: www.fed-soc.org
- Freedom's Watch: www.freedomswatch.org
- Heritage Foundation: www.heritage.org
- Hoover Institution: www.hoover.org
- Independent Women's Forum: www.iwf.org
- Leadership Institute: www.leadershipinstitute.org
- National Center for Constitutional Studies: www.nccs.net
- National Federation of Independent Business: www.nfib.com
- Young America's Foundation: www.yaf.org

NOTES

CHAPTER 1

1. Eric Hoffer, *The True Believer: Thoughts on the Nature of Mass Movements* (New York: Perennial, 1989), 109.

2. "Obama's inaugural speech," January 27, 2009; available at: www.cnn.com/2009/POLITICS/01/20/obama.politics/.

3. Associated Free Press, "'We have begun the work of remaking America:' Obama," April 28, 2009; available at: http://www.google.com/hostednews/afp/article/ALeqM5gBQgxxK38JyuSfg0w2DLlHsReieg.

4. "The Small Business Surtax," *Wall Street Journal*, July 14, 2009; available at: http://online.wsj.com/article/SB124753106668435899.html.

5. Alexander Tytler (Lord Woodhouselee, Alexander Fraser Tytler a Scottish historian/professor who wrote several books in the late 1700s and early 1800s), "The Fatal Sequence."

6. Ralph Waldo Emerson, "Society and Solitude," in *The Collected Works of Ralph Waldo Emerson,* vol. 7, ed. Douglas Emory Wilson (Cambridge, MA: Harvard University Press, 2007), 130.

7. W. Cleon Skousen, *The 5000 Year Leap: A Miracle That Changes the World,* 7th ed. (Malta, ID: National Center for Constitutional Studies, 1981), 121.

8. Ibid., 118.

9. National Center for Constitutional Studies; information available at: http://www.nccs.net/.

CHAPTER 2

1. Robert E. Rector, "How Poor Are America's Poor? Examining the 'Plague' of Poverty in America," Heritage Foundation, August 27, 2007; available at: http://www.heritage.org/Research/welfare/bg2064.cfm.

2. Ibid.

3. Dinesh D'Souza, *What's So Great About America?* (Washington, D.C.: Regnery Publishing, 2002), 76–77.

4. Presented by Celinda Lake, "The American Dream and the 2008 Election: Voters looking for leadership to restore the Dream"; data available at: http://www.changetowin.org/fileadmin/pdf/american-dream-sep-2007-lake-presentation.ppt.

5. "Voters Decide Between Free Markets and the Welfare State in 2008," *Trends Magazine,* January 2008; available at: http://www.trends-magazine.com/trend.php/Trend/1535/Category/56.

6. "The World's 25 Most Innovative Companies," *BusinessWeek*; available at: http://www.businessweek.com/pdfs/2006/0617_top25.pdf.

7. Ayn Rand, *Capitalism: The Unknown Ideal* (New York: The Penguin Group, 1967), 55.

8. "New Survey Shows U.S. Religious Giving to Developing Countries at $8.6 Billion," May 12, 2009; available at: http://www.hudson.org/index.cfm?fuseaction=publication_details&id=6237&pubType=HI_PressReleases.

9. "U.S. Financial Contributions to the United Nations System," September 20, 2007, U.S. Department of State Bureau of Public Affairs; available at: http://www.america.gov/st/texttrans-english/2007/September/20070924121555xjsnommiS6.101626e-02.html#ixzz0GZjgL7Ht&B (accessed November 5, 2009).

10. "ONE Says Expanded PEPFAR Means Renewed Life for Millions," United States & Aid to Africa Press Release, July 31, 2008; available at: http://www.one.org/c/us/pressrelease/32/.

11. Arthur Brooks, "A Nation of Givers," *The Journal of the American Enterprise Institute*, American Enterprise Institute, March/April 2008.

12. F. Scott Fitzgerald, "The Swimmers," quoted in Hyrum W. Smith, *What Matters Most: The Power of Living Your Values* (New York: Free Press, 2000), 14.

CHAPTER 3

1. Quoted in Adrienne Koch, *The American Enlightenment* (New York: George Braziller, Inc., 1965), 222.

2. Kurt Vonnegut, "Harrison Bergeron," 1961.

3. As quoted in Matthew Spalding, *We Still Hold These Truths* (Wilmington, DE: ISI Books, 2009), 203.

4. Eric Hoffer, *The True Believer: Thoughts on the Nature of Mass Movements*, 33 (omitting footnote in original).

5. Charles Sykes, *A Nation of Victims* (New York: St. Martin's Press, 1992).

6. Eric Hoffer, *The Passionate State of Mind* (New York: Buccaneer Books, 1955), 181.

7. Phil McGraw, *Life Strategies: Doing What Works, Doing What Matters* (New York: Hyperion Books, 1999), 76.

8. Ofer Zur, "Rethinking 'Don't Blame the Victim': The Psychology of Victimhood," Zur Institute, 1994; available at: http://www.zurinstitute.com/victimhood.html.

9. Thomas Jefferson, letter to John Adams, August 1, 1816; available at: http://oll.libertyfund.org/?option=com_staticxt&staticfile=show.php%3Ftitle=2127&chapter=193578&layout=html&Itemid=27.

10. Tommy Newberry, *366 Days of Wisdom & Inspiration*, Day 101 (Looking Glass Books, 1997).

11. "Obama hosts conference for Native American leaders," ABC News; available at: http://abcnews.go.com/Politics/president-obama-

hosts-conference-native-american-leaders-white/Story?id=8999579&
page=3.

CHAPTER 4

1. Ecclesiastes 30:24.

2. Tom Moore, "Overcoming Envy," The Preachers Files; available at: http://preachersfiles.com/overcoming-envy/.

3. Ronald Reagan, "Remarks at a Conservative Political Action Conference Dinner," February 26, 1982, National Archives and Records Administration, Public Papers of Ronald Reagan, Ronald Reagan Presidential Library; available at: http://www.reagan.utexas.edu/archives/speeches/1982/22682b.htm.

4. Barack Obama, "Sen. Barack Obama's Commencement Remarks," May 19, 2007, provided by SNHU Communications Office; available at: http://www.snhu.edu/6885.asp.

5. Ralph R. Reiland, "Michelle Obama's 'helping industry,'" *Pittsburgh Tribune-Review*, March 10, 2008; available at: http://www.pittsburghlive.com/x/pittsburghtrib/opinion/s_556214.html.

6. Michelle Malkin, *Culture of Corruption* (Washington, D.C.: Regnery Publishing, 2009).

7. Data available at: http://taxprof.typepad.com/taxprof_blog/2009/04/obama-and-biden-release-tax-returns.html.

8. John McCormick, "White House wealth: President Barack Obama's Team virtually all Chicago millionaires," *Chicago Tribune*, April 9, 2009; available at: http://www.chicagotribune.com/news/politics/obama/chi-white-house-wealthapr09,0,1573304.story.

9. Michelle Malkin, *Culture of Corruption*, 170.

10. Jonah Goldberg, "For the Common Good," The Corner, *National Review Online*, June 29, 2004; available at: http://corner.nationalreview.com/post/?q=YmExYzVjYTY1ZTJiODA0YmY2NGI2ZDU0Yzg0ODZjMDE=.

11. Robert Reich, "The House: Tax the Wealthy to Keep Everyone Healthy," Robert Reich's Blog, July 15, 2009; available at: http://robertreich.blogspot.com/2009/07/house-tax-wealthy-to-keep-everyone.html.

12. "Transcript: the Vice-Presidential Debate," Election 2008, *New York Times*, October 2, 2008; available at: http://elections.nytimes.com/2008/president/debates/transcripts/vice-presidential-debate.html.

13. Larry Elder, "Hard Work Wins...Still," *World Net Daily*, December 9, 2004; available at: http://70.85.195.205/news/printer-friendly.asp?ARTICLE_ID=41846.

14. Johannes von Goethe, *Proverbs in Prose* (1819).

15. Data available at *Fiscal Facts*, The Tax Foundation, http://www.taxfoundation.org/research/show/250.html.

16. "Remarks By the President On International Tax Policy Reform," The White House, Office of the Press Secretary, May 4, 2009; available at: http://www.whitehouse.gov/the_press_office/Remarks-By-The-President-On-International-Tax-Policy-Reform.

17. Barack Obama, Chicago Public Radio, January 18, 2001; full transcript available at: http://www.foxnews.com/urgent_queue/#50041ecb,2008-10-27.

18. "Joe the Plumber 'The Whole Conversation,'" posted October 16, 2008; available at: http://www.youtube.com/watch?v=8Ilwk_wmsQk.

19. Quote taken from "Thomas Jefferson on Politics and Government," Property Rights; available at: http://etext.virginia.edu/jefferson/quotations/jeff1550.htm.

20. Abraham Lincoln, "Reply to New York Workingmen's Democratic Republican Association, March 21, 1864," in *The Collected Works of Abraham Lincoln*, vol. 7, ed. Roy P. Basler (New Brunswick, NJ:Rutgers University Press, 1990), 259–60.

21. Arthur Laffer and Stephen Moore, "Soak the Rich, Lose the Rich," *Wall Street Journal*, May 18, 2009; available at: http://online.wsj.com/article/SB124260067214828295.html.

22. Ibid.

23. "Millionaires Go Missing," *Wall Street Journal*, May 27, 2009; available at: http://online.wsj.com/article/SB124329282377252471.html.

24. Christina D. Romer and David H. Romer, "The Macroeconomic Effect of Tax Changes: Estimates Based on a New Measure of Fiscal Shocks," University of California, Berkeley, March 2007; available at: http://elsa.berkeley.edu/~cromer/RomerDraft307.pdf.

25. J. D. Foster, "Tax Hikes, Economic Clouds, and Silver Linings: A Review of Deficits and the Economy," The Heritage Foundation, February 25, 2008; available online at: http://www.heritage.org/Research/Taxes/bg2095.cfm.

26. P. J. O'Rourke, "An Alternative Inaugural Address," *The Weekly Standard*, January 18, 2005; available at: http://www.weeklystandard.com/Content/Public/Articles/000/000/005/141kgagb.asp.

CHAPTER 5

1. Cal Thomas, "Can't do spirit," *Insight Magazine*, June 19, 2008.

2. "Sellers of 'Fat Trapper Plus' and 'Exercise in a Bottle' Banned from Advertising Weight-Loss Products," Federal Trade Commission, January 18, 2005; available at: http://www.ftc.gov/opa/2005/01/enforma.shtm.

3. "Couch Potatoes Rejoice: Scientists Say 'Exercise in a Pill' Possible to Fight Obesity, Diabetes," Fox News, July 31, 2008; available at: http://www.foxnews.com/story/0,2933,395321,00.html.

4. Interview with Craig Snyder, colleague and mentee of Dr. Adrian Rogers, August 14, 2009.

5. *Good Morning America*, ABC, September 18, 2008; See also "Biden calls paying higher taxes a patriotic act"; transcript available at: http://www.msnbc.msn.com/id/26771716/.

6. Data available at: http://taxprof.typepad.com/taxprof_blog/2009/04/obama-and-biden-release-tax-returns.html. Source: IRS.

7. Barack Obama Commencement Address at Knox College, June 4, 2005; video and transcript of speech available at: http://deptorg.knox.edu/newsarchive/news_events/2005/x9683.html.

8. Linda Bowles, "The Weaning Process," *Washington Times*, December 20, 1994, p. A16

9. Joel Bleifuss, "A Politically Correct Lexicon," *In These Times*, February 21, 2007; available at: http://www.inthesetimes.com/article/3027/a_politically_correct_lexicon/.

10. For more information on the Frankfurt School, see: http://www.marxists.org/subject/frankfurt-school/index.htm.

11. Theodore Roosevelt on Immigration, 1907.

12. "America's Best Days," Rasmussen Reports, November 5, 2009; available at: http://www.rasmussenreports.com/public_content/politics/mood_of_america/america_s_best_days.

13. Ibid.

14. "Poll Shows Support for Official English at New High," Zogby International, March 21, 2006; available at: http://www.zogby.com/soundbites/readclips.cfm?ID=12892.

15. 1,000 likely voters were polled by Rasmussen Reports, June 17–18. 2005. The margin of error was +/- 3%. Data available at: http://www.proenglish.org/resources/polls.html.

16. 1,002 foreign-born adults were polled in the fall of 2002 by the Carnegie Corporation of New York. The margin of error was +/- 3%.

17. 3,000 Hispanic adults were polled by the Pew Hispanic Center in December, 2002. The margin of error was +/- 2.41%.

18. Mark Steyn, "You Feelin' Hucky?" *New York Sun*, January 7, 2008; available at: http://www.nysun.com/opinion/you-feelin-hucky/69011/.

19. Fergie, "Where is the Love" lyrics.

20. Robert Spencer, *Stealth Jihad* (Washington, D.C.: Regnery, 2008), 91–92.

21. Daniel Zwerdling and Steve Inskeep, "Former Colleagues Say Hasan Was Detached," National Public Radio, November 10, 2009; available at: http://www.npr.org/templates/story/story.php?storyId=120266836.

22. Agustin Blazquez and Jaums Sutton, "Political Correctness: The Scourge of Our Times," Newsmax.com, April 8, 2002; available at: http://archive.newsmax.com/archives/articles/2002/4/4/121115.shtml.

CHAPTER 6

1. Walter Lippmann, *An Inquiry Into the Principles of the Good Society* (Boston: Little and Brown, 1937), 3–6.

2. Saul Alinsky, *Rules for Radicals: A Pragmatic Primer for Realistic Radicals* (New York: Random House, 1971).

3. John Stuart Mill, "Individuality As One of the Elements of Wellbeing," in *On Liberty*; text available at: http://books.google.com/books?id=f14SAAAAIAAJ&dq=John+Stuart+Mill,+%E2%80%9CIndividuality+As+One+of+the+Elements+of+Wellbeing,%E2%80%9D+in+On+Liberty&printsec=frontcover&source=bn&hl=en&ei=uccGS6H-D8qslAfU77iFBA&sa=X&oi=book_result&ct=result&resnum=5&ved=0CBYQ6AEwBA#v=onepage&q=&f=false.

4. Barack Obama, *Dreams from My Father* (New York: Three Rivers Press, 2004).

5. Lydia Saad, "Political Ideology: 'Conservative' Label Prevails in the South," Gallup, August 14, 2009; available at: http://www.gallup.com/poll/122333/Political-Ideology-Conservative-Label-Prevails-South.aspx.

6. Ibid.

7. Thomas G. West and William A. Schambra, "The Progressive Movement and the Transformation of American Politics," #12 in the First Principles Series, Heritage Foundation, July 18, 2007; available at: http://www.heritage.org/Research/Thought/fp12.cfm.

8. Ibid.

9. Frank Johnson Goodnow, *The American Conception of Liberty and Government* (Providence, RI: Standard Printing Company, 1916), 11.

10. Ronald J. Pestritto, "The Birth of the Administrative State: Where It Came From and What It Means for Limited Government," #16 in the First Principles Series, Heritage Foundation, November 20, 2007; available at: http://www.heritage.org/Research/Thought/fp16.cfm.

11. Matthew Spalding, *We Still Hold These Truths*, 203.

12. Ibid., 194.

13. Thomas G. West and William A. Schambra, "The Progressive Movement and the Transformation of American Politics," #12 in the First Principles Series, Heritage Foundation, July 18, 2007.

14. Ibid.

15. Woodrow Wilson, *The State* (Boston: D.C. Heath, 1889), 651.

16. Thomas Jefferson, "A Noiseless Course," Letter to Thomas Cooper, November 29, 1802 (Charlottesville, VA: Electronic Text Center, University of Virginia Library); available at: http://etext.virginia.edu/

etcbin/toccer-new2?id=JefLett.sgm&images=images/modeng&data=/
texts/english/modeng/parsed&tag=public&part=147&division=div1.

17. Thomas G. West and William A. Schambra, "The Progressive Movement and the Transformation of American Politics," #12 in the First Principles Series, Heritage Foundation, July 18, 2007.

18. Ronald J. Pestritto, "The Birth of the Administrative State: Where It Came From and What It Means for Limited Government," #16 in the First Principles Series, Heritage Foundation, November 20, 2007.

19. Victor Davis Hanson, "The Ugly—Part Two," Pajamas Media, March 28, 2009; available at: http://www.victorhanson.com/articles/hanson032809.html.

20. C. S. Lewis, *The Screwtape Letters*, 1942.

21. "European Malaise," *Trends* Magazine, November 2007; available at: http://www.trends-magazine.com/trend.php/Trend/1495/Category/45.

22. Marcus Walker, "Sweden Clamps Down on Sick and Disability Pay," *Wall Street Journal,* May 9, 2007.

23. "European Malaise," *Trends* Magazine, November 2007.

24. Peter Millar, "Trouble in Welfare Paradise," *The Sunday Times*, September 17, 2006.

25. Marcus Walker, "Sweden Clamps Down on Sick and Disability Pay," *The Wall Street Journal,* May 9, 2007.

26. Martin Wolf, "There is Something Rotten in the Welfare State of Europe," *Financial Times*, March 1, 2006.

27. Corinne Maier, *Bonjour Laziness* (New York: Pantheon Books, 2005).

28. "European Malaise," *Trends* Magazine, November 2007.

29. Dick Morris and Eileen McGann, "The Nobel Prize to Obama: Europe's Bid to Re-colonize America," October 9, 2009; available at: http://www.dickmorris.com/blog/2009/10/09/the-nobel-prize-to-obama-europes-bid-to-re-colonize-america/.

30. "Media Bias Basics: How the Media Vote"; data available at: http://www.mrc.org/biasbasics/biasbasics3.asp.

31. "Press Accuracy Ratings Hits Two Decade Low," Pew Research Center for the People and the Press, September 13, 2009; data available at: http://people-press.org/report/543/.

32. "Majority Say Reporters Tried to Help Obama," Rasmussen Reports, November 4, 2008; data available at: http://www.rasmussenreports.com/public_content/politics/elections2/election_20082/2008_presidential_election/majority_say_reporters_tried_to_help_obama.

33. David A. Noebel, "How the Socialists Are Destroying America From Within," *Hot Air*, May 16, 2009; available at: http://hotair.com/greenroom/archives/2009/05/16/david-a-noebel-how-the-socialist-are-destroying-america-from-within/.

34. "Ronald Reagan Speaks Out on Socialized Medicine," posted by The Reagan Foundation, July 23, 2009; video available at: http://www.youtube.com/watch?v=AYrlDlrLDSQ&feature=player_embedded#.

35. Victor Davis Hanson, "The Ugly—Part Two," Pajamas Media, March 28, 2009; available at: http://www.victorhanson.com/articles/hanson032809.html.

CHAPTER 7

1. Frank Newport, "This Easter, Smaller Percentage of Americans Are Christian," Gallup Poll, April 10, 2009; available at: http://www.gallup.com/poll/117409/easter-smaller-percentage-americans-christian.aspx.

2. Genesis 1: 1–31.

3. Ibid.

4. Romans 2:10; 3:23; 5:12; 5:19.

5. Genesis 3:12–13.

6. Johan Norberg, *In Defense of Global Capitalism* (Washington, D.C.: The Cato Institute, 2003), 17.

7. Napoleon Hill, *Law of Success* (Hammond, IN: Napoleon Hill Foundation, 1979), 82.

8. Leviticus 5–6.

9. Saul D. Alinsky, *Rules for Radicals* (New York: Vintage Books, 1972).

10. St. Francis de Sales, *Introduction to the Devout Life*, as quoted in Fr. Robert Sirico, "Catholics for Marx," *Front Page Magazine* Online; available at: http://97.74.65.51/readArticle.aspx?ARTID=12826.

11. Genesis 23:12–20 (NIV).

12. Richard Theodore Ely, *Recent American Socialism*, Vol. 3, 1888, pg. 9.

13. David Boaz, "Private Property Saved Jamestown and, With It, America," Grassroot Institute of Hawaii, June 26, 2007; available at: http://www.grassrootinstitute.org/system/old/GrassrootPerspective/Jamestown.shtml.

14. Richard J. Maybury, "The Great Thanksgiving Hoax," Mises Daily, November 20, 1999; available at: http://mises.org/daily/336.

15. Ibid.; see also: William Bradford, *Bradford's History of the Plymouth Settlement* (New York: E.P. Dutton & Co.), 115 in Note 16.

16. William Bradford, *Bradford's History of The Plymouth Settlement*, 115.

17. Ibid.

18. 1 Kings 3:5–13

19. Job 1:1–3

20. Job 42:12–17

21. Bert Thompson, "The Case for the Existence of God, Part II," ApologeticsPress.org, 1995; available at: http://www.apologeticspress.org/articles/2518.

22. Ibid.; see also: William Beck, *Human Design* (New York: Harcourt, Brace, Jovanovich, 1971), 189.

23. Proverbs 14:23.

24. Ecclesiastes 9:10.

25. 1 Corinthians 10:31 CEV.

26. Proverbs 16:3.

27. Ephesians 4:25 AMP.

28. Proverbs 19:24 NKJV.

29. Proverbs 22:29 NKJV.

30. Proverbs 21:5 NKJV.

31. Proverbs 20:13 NKJV.

32. Proverbs 21:15 NKJV.

33. 2 Thessalonians 3:7–14.

34. Karl Marx quoted in William Beck, *Human Design.*

35. Thomas Jefferson, "Notes on the State of Virginia"; available at: http://www.interviewwithgod.com/patriotic/quotes.htm.

36. Henry Van Dyke, quote in *Fisherman's Luck.*

37. Leviticus 19:18; Matthew 22:39 (NIV).

38. Matthew 7:24–27.

CHAPTER 8

1. Ralph Waldo Emerson, "The American Scholar"; text available at: http://www.vcu.edu/engweb/transcendentalism/authors/emerson/essays/amscholar.htm.

2. James Allen, in Andy Zubko, ed., *The Wisdom of James Allen*, 25.

3. Thomas J. Stanley, Ph.D, and William D. Danko, Ph.D., "Meet the Millionaire Next Door," chapter 1 in *The Millionaire Next Door: The Surprising Secrets of America's Wealthy*, *New York Times* books; available at: http://www.nytimes.com/books/first/s/stanley-millionaire.html.

4. Ibid.

5. "The Forbes 400," ed. Matthew Miller and Duncan Greenberg, Forbes.com, September 17, 2008; available at: http://www.forbes.com/2008/09/16/forbes-400-billionaires-lists-400list08_cx_mn_0917richamericans_land.html.

6. Geoffrey Colvin, "What it takes to be great," *Fortune*, October 19, 2006; available at: http://money.cnn.com/magazines/fortune/fortune_archive/2006/10/30/8391794/index.htm.

7. Ibid.

8. "The 2004 Political Landscape," Pew Research Center; available at: http://people-press.org/report/?pageid=753.

9. "America's Best Days," Rasmussen Reports, November 5, 2009; available at: http://www.rasmussenreports.com/public_content/politics/mood_of_america/america_s_best_days.

10. Biography of Hobby Lobby CEO David Green, ChristiaNet; available at: http://christiannews.christianet.com/1096289115.htm.

11. Andria Cheng, "Home Depot to lower 10% of headquarters staff," *Market Watch*, January 31, 2008; available at: http://www. marketwatch.com/story/home-depot-to-lower-10-of-headquarters-staff.

12. Napoleon Hill, *Law of Success* (Napoleon Hill Foundation, 1979), 121.

13. Myron Magnet, *The Dream and the Nightmare: The Sixties' Legacy to the Underclass* (New York: William Morrow and Company, 1993), 19.

14. James Allen in Andy Zubko, ed., *The Wisdom of James Allen* (Laurel Creek Press, 1987), 20.

15. Thomas Sowell, "The Great Escape," *Human Events*, August 25, 2009; available at: http://www.humanevents.com/article.php?id=33264.

16. Karl Eller, Executive MBA Announcement, Eller Executive MBA : Eller College of Management, November 10, 2007; available at: http:// www.eller.arizona.edu/docs/press/2007/11/KarlEller_EMBA_ Convocation_Nov10_2007.pdf

CHAPTER 9

1. Blaise Pascal, *Pensees (Thoughts)*, No. 119; quoted in Tommy Newberry, *366 Days of Wisdom and Inspiration* (Mason Press), Day 256.

2. Matthew 13:3–8.

3. This quote from Epicletus is quoted in Tommy Newberry, *366 Days of Wisdom and Inspiration*, Day 50.

4. Henry Wadsworth Longfellow, "The Ladder of Saint Augustine," lines 37–40, in *The Poetical Works of Henry Wadsworth Longfellow*, Riverside Edition (Boston: Houghton Mifflin, 1890).

5. James Allen, in Andy Zubko, ed., *The Wisdom of James Allen*, 27.

6. Napoleon Hill, *Law of Success* (Napoleon Hill Foundation, 1979), 58.

7. Andy Stanley, *The Principle of the Path: How to Get from Where You Are to Where You Want to Be* (Nashville, TN: Thomas Nelson, 2009).

8. Steven R. Covey, January 17 in *Daily Reflections for Highly Effective People: Living the 7 Habits of Highly Effective People Every Day* (Franklin Covey Co., 1994).

9. Brian Tracy, "Building Your Network," Brian Tracy International, March 25, 2008; available at: http://www.briantracy.com/articles/default.aspx?topicid=9&dtd=20080325.

10. Sam Walton, *The Business Book of Wisdom*, ed. Peter Krass (Hoboken, NJ: Wiley & Sons, 1997), 229.

11. Earl Nightingale, *The Essence of Success* (Niles, IL: Nightingale Conant Corporation, 1993), 444

12. Urban Dictionary, "Stupid," http://www.urbandictionary.com/define.php?term=stupid.

13. Friedrich A. Hayek, *The Road to Serfdom* (Chicago: University of Chicago Press, 1972).

CHAPTER 10

1. Mack J. Casner, "Winning the Cultural War: Charlton Heston at Harvard Law School in 1999," in *Rules for Conservatives: A Cultural War Guide* (Booklocker.com, Inc., 2009), 10.

2. "About the Fairtax," Americans for Fair Taxation; available at: http://www.fairtax.org/site/PageServer?pagename=about_main.

3. Walter Williams, *Liberty Versus the Tyranny of Socialism* (Stanford, CA: Hoover Institution Press, 2008), 152.

4. Karl Rove, "The President's Apology Tour," *Wall Street Journal*, April 23, 2009; also available at: http://online.wsj.com/article/SB124044156269345357.html.

5. Thomas Paine, "The Crisis I," in *The American Crisis* (Radford, VA: Wilder Publications, 2007), 9.

6. Ibid, 7.

INDEX